LOVE LOST, LOVE FOUND

LOVE LOST, LOVE FOUND

A WOMAN'S GUIDE TO LETTING GO OF THE PAST AND FINDING NEW LOVE

TATIANA JEROME

New World Library
Novato, California

New World Library
14 Pamaron Way
Novato, California 94949

Text design by Tona Pearce Myers

Library of Congress Cataloging-in-Publication Data
Names: Jerome, Tatiana, [date]– author.
Title: Love lost, love found : a woman's guide to letting go of the past and
    finding new love / Tatiana Jerome.
Description: Novato, California : New World Library, [2017]
Identifiers: LCCN 2016045872 (print) | LCCN 2017001743 (ebook) | ISBN
    9781608684779 (alk. paper) | ISBN 9781608684786 (Ebook)
Subjects: LCSH: Man-woman relationships. | Man-woman relationships—
    Religious aspects—Christianity. | Single women. | Interpersonal relations.
    | Love.
Classification: LCC HQ801 .J47 2017 (print) | LCC HQ801 (ebook) | DDC
    306.7—dc23
LC record available at https://lccn.loc.gov/2016045872

First printing, March 2017
ISBN 978-1-60868-477-9
Ebook ISBN 978-1-60868-478-6

Printed in the USA on 100% postconsumer-waste recycled paper

New World Library is proud to be a Gold Certified Environmentally
Responsible Publisher. Publisher certification awarded by Green Press
Initiative. www.greenpressinitiative.org

10   9   8   7   6   5   4   3   2   1

Dedicated to Every Queen

I dedicate this book to every woman who ever wanted
to feel free. I dedicate the heart of this book to every
woman who believes in love and knows that it belongs to her because it is her.

CONTENTS

ACKNOWLEDGMENT

You gave me a voice, your spirit, love, forgiveness, and peace, and for that I give you my many todays and my countless forevers.

 # PREFACE

Things seemed to be going okay. So what if he didn't put down the toilet seat? So what if he couldn't seem to pick me up on time or hadn't made any real plans with me? Nobody's perfect, right? No one has a perfect relationship. We had a good time, for the most part. In our three-year relationship, the good outweighed the bad. We moved in together partly because he was about to be evicted, and I wanted to be there for him. I also thought it would make us grow closer. I like to go out from time to time, and he likes to stay home. So we compromised. We would go to a movie every now and then, but mostly we'd stay home. I would cook us a meal, and you know, one thing led to another, and we would knock out. I wouldn't really call that a date, but it was time with my love.

Overall, things were good, and much better than they were in my last relationship, which was long-distance (well, not really long-distance; he was just two hours away, but he hardly ever came to see me). I was used to seeing him about once every two months, and he rarely wanted to talk on the phone. When I did speak to him, he really didn't have much to say, and he never asked about me. So this was much better. I was happy — until the day my partner called from work to say he wanted to end things.

I spent the first three hours after that call trying to figure out why. The only thing he could tell me is that things weren't working out. He said he had asked me time and time again to change certain things but that I never did. He said I nag too much, that I'm not down for him, that I'm always trying to start trouble. It was hard for me to think, and I couldn't stop my tears. "Are you serious?" That's all that came to mind to say. He ended the conversation by telling me I'm not who I used to be. He said he would come and get his things when I was at work. I can't even say I was shocked. It's not like we hadn't broken up before. It's not like we hadn't done the whole break-up-to-make-up thing. But it's been more than a month, and I haven't heard from him. I guess it's really over.

LADIES, IF THIS IS YOU, STOP RIGHT HERE!!

Maybe you're thinking, wait, that can't be the whole story — I want to know the details! Maybe I can relate to them! You might even be saying, "Well, at least he was better than your ex." Ugh. I'm here to tell you right now, stop that kind of thinking. Just stop it. The details do *not* matter, and they never will. Just as you learned in school, there's the main idea, and then there's the details to support the main idea. Well, the main idea has already played out. It's over. The only person holding on to the details of your relationship is you, because you want answers. If he cared about the details, then splitting up would have been a topic of discussion rather than a unilateral choice — his.

The details do not matter. All the things you did for him do not matter. Your sacrifices do not matter. They did not make a strong enough impact on his choice. Yes, you don't throw away a relationship without trying to fix it first, but, and this is a big but, if you're the only one trying to fix it, it will never work out. If there was never a place for God in the relationship, then there was never any room for solutions to your problems to present themselves.

If You Ended It Because You Know Your Worth, This Part Is for You

---

If you are the one who ended it, then congratulations. It was probably one of the hardest things you've ever had to do. You didn't want to end it — but maybe secretly you did. Maybe the relationship wasn't always this bad, but it also wasn't getting any better. It was clear you were being taken for granted, that you were being used as a backup plan or a safety net by your partner. You were no longer considered a gift to him. So you did what you had to do, and you ended it. You said good-bye — or did you really? Did you say good-bye and then end all communication with him? On social media, email, and so forth? Or did you say good-bye without really believing it had ended?

Just because you were the one to let go doesn't mean it doesn't hurt. Maybe you felt relief at removing yourself from the situation, but that doesn't mean the pain is gone. That doesn't make it any easier to deal with, so this is your time to mourn. This is your time to figure out what's next. It's not your time to figure out what to do if he contacts you. It's not your time to figure out if he's thinking about you. You are only delaying the healing process. You are allowed to let the tears run. You are allowed to feel pain, hurt, anger, and disappointment. You are allowed to miss him, but that doesn't mean you have to go back. No one said letting go would be easy, but now you are no longer tied to a toxic situation.

The Thing Is, You Knew It Was Going to Happen

Somewhere inside you, you knew. You knew the relationship was going to end, because it was going against your spirit. If you really took the time to search within yourself, over time you'd realize that you knew this was not right for you and that things had to come to an end. You knew you had to let go. You knew you couldn't change things or him. You knew things were not going to get better.

Your spirit tells you when people and situations no longer serve you or are detrimental to you. You can either take heed and listen from within, or you can negotiate and make excuses for what the spirit knows and sees. The longer you prolong the process of letting go, the louder your spirit becomes, trying to protect itself from being silenced and you from being stuck, no longer able to make the best decisions for yourself. I always say the connection you have with someone happens when two spirits meet before you physically do, and by the same token, your spirit knows how to guide you in the right direction, if only you would listen to it instead of questioning it. Your spirit knows when to accept what is beneficial to you and when to reject what is harmful.

If you haven't been listening to your spirit for quite some time, it may have taken you longer to notice what you should've seen earlier. Regardless of what has happened, you are an intelligent woman who knows when things are not headed in the right direction. You are able to see that what he once did to attract you, he no longer does. You are aware of the excuses being made. You are keen to his next "I don't know," "I don't have the time," "I'm focused on making money," "I'm focused on doing what I have to do," and "I'm not ready." You knew it was only a matter of time before things had to end. Within you . . . you knew. You may not have acknowledged it, but you knew. All the signs were there. Everything that told you to end it, such as body language, was clear. You asked God for a sign, and he gave you more than one. It was just a matter of time before you did something about it, after you overcame your fears, the "what-ifs," and the memories, good and bad. The time came to choose better treatment, to choose love and support over indifference and maybe even mistreatment. You're probably experiencing a range of emotions, from wanting him back, to asking yourself if ending it was really the right choice, to thinking maybe you were too drastic, to believing you're better off without him, to feeling sad and wondering if all these feelings will ever go away.

When God is present within you, he will protect you. He will provide for you, and he is waiting for you to look to him for all your answers and to be patient about the process of healing. You are seeking God, and he is there.

You Made a Decision, So Now What?

Now it's time for you to stick to your decision. There is no looking back. There are no what-ifs. *Right now* is what you have. Your present and your future are the only things you can invest in. Your decision to move forward is what's best for *you* (and if you have kids, then it's best for them too). Your decision indicates that far from being lost, you are more than capable of making healthy choices to get you to a better place. Remember, you didn't always feel like this. You weren't always wondering "What now?" and feeling pain. You once felt joy and excitement about what was to come, and, most important, you felt loved. You can and will feel those things again. There is *no doubt* about that, and no doubt that you will take the path required to get you there. Your current feelings will not last forever. Right now, put your relationship with God, and yourself, first. Right now, get back to tending to yourself and making your feelings, needs, and wants a priority. Right now, start believing that better days are here. You are already in a better place, because you made a decision. You are already starting to heal. So put the things of the past behind you. Put your excuses behind you, and put his excuses behind you too. It's truly time to heal.

Healing May Not Happen Right Away

There is always a choice between truly healing and staying stuck in pain. When you truly heal, you are open to possibilities. You allow God to use you. Your focus remains on God and your relationship with him. You feel strong enough to achieve your goals. You are genuinely in a happier place. Healing enables you to attract like-minded people. You think and talk about doing better and being better. You are uplifting to others, and most important, you love yourself ten times more. You work on your shortcomings and expect improvement. You bring forth better opportunities and summon love to enter your life. Your spirit becomes more attractive, and your presence is welcomed.

When you don't truly heal, you stay stuck in pain. You become too guarded, and by that I mean that you are not approachable or open-minded to God's way of bringing what is divine and right for you. You focus on the negative things that could happen and function out of fear. You make excuses about why good things cannot happen for you. You make assumptions about people and situations. When you are still angry inside, and pushing people away from you, you are not really healing. You are envious of other people's happiness, and you expect disappointment instead of success. Responding to a breakup this way is not true healing but rather a way to stay bruised and isolated from any blessing.

Your healing process is a very delicate time. To truly heal requires time and patience. It's time to get back to happy, get back to *love*, and start this whole process over the right way.

THE FUNDAMENTAL CAN'TS

The moment you start thinking about all the things you did wrong in your relationship, all the things you should have said and done, should have done differently, and should have spotted before they happened, is the moment you've decided to put yourself through misery. Yes, taking responsibility is a big part of the healing process, but failing to recognize his shortcomings and making excuses for him only keeps you in a state of denial.

Whether you allowed him to make you feel a certain way about the state of your relationship or you are choosing to protect his reputation, the fundamental truth is, you only have control over your own actions and words. While certain actions can evoke a variety of responses, both verbal and physical, you cannot control or take the full blame for the demise of the relationship, and nor should you want to. When you do this, you are essentially letting him off the hook and downplaying his role in helping the relationship come to an end.

Even if you decide to examine every single detail of your previous relationship (and I advise against it!), there are a few fundamental can'ts that you should always keep in mind when moving forward in your healing.

1. YOU CAN'T MAKE A MAN FALL IN LOVE WITH YOU. No matter how strong your feelings are for him or how well you cook and clean and love all over him, you cannot make a man fall in love with you. If he is not ready to love you, there is nothing you can do to change that. The amount of energy you used to give to catering to your partner should now be redirected to loving and respecting yourself.

2. YOU CAN'T CHANGE A MAN. Change happens within a person when something tragic occurs, when something amazing happens, or when a person simply wants to change. You cannot nag, beg, or manipulate change to happen in someone else. Any change that occurs within a person, good or bad, is of that person's own doing. If he willingly makes the effort to change an attribute of his behavior to improve himself, it is because he wants to, not because he was forced to.

3. YOU CAN'T BELIEVE EVERYTHING YOU'RE TOLD. Words are just that...words. Without actions to

support them, they mean nothing. If someone tells you he loves you but never acts lovingly toward you, why would you believe him? If someone says she is sorry but continues to do the same things for which she claimed she was sorry, how can you believe she is truly sorry? Remember that words market, but action sells.

4. YOU CAN'T RELY ON A SINGLE ACTION. Yes, I know I just said that actions sell, but I'm going to add that actions do not matter as much as patterns. After all, a person can do something once or twice and then choose to stop. It's when actions become a pattern that they really matter. An action that has become a pattern is known as a habit, good or bad. So if he does something for the first time, such as waving his hand in front of your face when he makes a point, and you laugh it off, then he can decide to make a habit out of it. If the first time you step off a sidewalk to cross the street in your five-inch heels he grabs your hand, and you give him a favorable reaction, he can decide to do this again and again until it becomes a habit. But if he does these things once or twice and no more, then you cannot make a judgment call about his true behavior.

5. YOU CAN'T STOP BEING YOU. When you're in a relationship, you should never stop being yourself. Many women who do this fail to realize that their guy met them and liked them for who they are (or at least who they presented themselves to be). Taking on someone

else's identity rather than being true to yourself has negative effects not only on your self-esteem but also on your relationships with your family and friends. You should always have interests outside your relationship and continue to improve yourself as an individual.

2 THE ROLLER COASTER OF REACTIONS

Most breakups come with a series of feelings that dictate how we act and that essentially shape our day. You may feel happy one minute and upset the next when a sudden memory from your past relationship floats up. It's okay to feel these feelings. But remember that you base your reactions to situations and people on how you are feeling. Your feelings are just a mirror of the beliefs you hold about your past relationship; how you feel is based on what you believed the relationship was supposed to be. These feelings are not something that can be brushed away, but with a bit of work they can certainly be tamed. Below is a list of emotions you have probably felt at one time or another or are currently feeling:

ANGRY. Who does he think he is? I can't believe he never apologized. Now he wants to play the victim after everything I've done for him, after all the things I overlooked and forgave him for. My family warned me about him. I lowered my standards in order to date him. I mean, I didn't really want to be with him in the beginning, and this is how he repays me? It's one lie after another. All I did was love him. This is how he is going to treat me? He had no respect for me or this relationship. I put up with so much to make this thing between us work, and all he can think about is his needs. He acts as if he is the only one who matters in this relationship. So everything about our relationship was a lie. Was nothing real to him? How can he be so selfish?

CONFUSED. Is it really over? How did we even get here? Everything was good just a week ago. I thought we were on the same page but just reading it in different languages. I just met his mom and his best friend. What was that all about? Why did he tell me I was his forever? How can he say he loves me but then put all these other things and people before us? Before me? Why did I cry more than I laughed in this relationship? One minute he tells me he knows what he wants, and the next he's saying we're moving too fast. I never asked him to be anyone but himself, and now I'm seeing a whole different person. He told me to wait for him, but now he can't wait for me? He knew who I was and what I was about before we got together, so why is he acting like he can't handle it now?

STUPID. He made such a fool of me in front of our families and friends. I can't believe I let it last this long. I should have been the one to end this relationship. I knew better. I knew the whole time. I refused to listen to anybody but him. I stood up for him, and yet he never changed. He disrespected me and treated my feelings like they were nothing. I should have trusted my intuition. He really thinks I'm that dumb. He's been saying the same thing for so long, and I continued to believe in him. I can't believe I let him play me. Every time he asked for something, I said yes, even when I was too tired or too sick to do it. I made so many sacrifices to help him, no questions asked, and this is the thanks I get. I knew he couldn't be trusted, and I still said yes. I let my guard down for this? For him? What was I thinking?

INDIFFERENT. Here we go again. This is nothing new. I'm over it. It was going to happen anyway. It is what it is. I don't have time to think about him. I have so many other things to focus on. If he calls, he calls; if he doesn't, whatever. It's not like he was my soul mate. I saw this coming but just didn't expect it to happen now. He'll be back. This isn't the first time we've broken up. He always comes back with an excuse. I'm used to this. I'm used to him acting like this. I'm always the mature one in this relationship. It's gotten to the point where I just let him be. I know I can't change him, so I don't even say anything. I don't have the strength for this or for him.

HAPPY. This is finally over. What a mess I was in! I'm no longer stuck. I feel like a huge weight has been lifted off my shoulders. I knew I was too good for him. I was too good for that relationship. It was only a matter of time before it came to an end. I can finally move on. I can get back to me. I am in the zone and working on being happy. I get to attend to my needs instead of putting his before mine. I feel like I'm winning. I'm in a good place. This is a different kind of happy. There are no conditions to my happiness now. I feel at peace now. I now know what I want. I know what I want love to look like in my life. I thank God for removing what no longer serves me. I had been holding on way too long, but God rescued me.

EXCITED. I can't wait to see what the future holds. I'm going to work on all the things I want to improve so that my next relationship will be a hundred times better. I have so much hope and excitement about all the amazing people I'm going to meet. I know I'm ready. I will finally put myself in a real relationship that provides mutual support and love. I can finally take the time to love me and accomplish my goals without wondering what he's up to. I can sleep at night, knowing that no one is playing games with my heart. I'm putting myself in a place to be in a real relationship with someone who will pray with me and for us. I'll put myself in a position where not only will I feel love, but everyone will be able to see our love and not just our issues. I don't need to try to get back together for the eighth time. I get a fresh, new start. I no longer have to worry about him, and he doesn't need to worry about me. I want only to wish him the best.

CRAZY. Oh, so he thinks he can end it like this? He doesn't know all the stuff I know about him. I will terrorize him. He doesn't know me. He thought it was bad before; well, wait till he sees how much worse it's about to get. He'd better not be talking to another female on Facebook. He'd better pick up when I call him. I should stop by his workplace and let everyone know what kind of man he really is. I'm protecting all women from men like him. I miss him. Maybe we can work this out. I probably didn't hear right. Nah, that bastard deserves to feel what I'm feeling. I need to let him know exactly who I think he is. I'm going to keep calling till he picks up. Oh, his voice mailbox is full; well, I'll just hit him up on iMessenger.

DEFEATED. Why didn't I see this coming? I mean, I knew it wasn't going to work out. I should never have texted him. Why do I even feel this way? I never make good choices. I never should have told him I loved him. I never should have lent him money. I never received a thank-you for half the things I did. I mean, why can't he just call me back? What did I ever do to him that he should treat me like this? He always told me I never got it. I was never really his "it" girl. I believed him when he told me to wait on him. When he didn't come home or call me back, I gave him the benefit of the doubt. I'm the one who needs help.

Understanding Your Feelings and Taking Control

Breakups can bring up every emotion in the book, and we've all been through them. One minute you're just fine, and the next you feel like your world just came tumbling down. The heartache you're feeling just cannot compare to anything else you've felt (outside of something really tragic). You feel alone. Even your ex can't seem to understand your pain. The people around you say they understand and keep telling you that it will get better, but you just can't take in what they are saying. You want to know when. Sometimes, you may even subconsciously enjoy the pain, because it's the only way you feel you can stay connected to your ex. Even during this roller-coaster ride, you feel like you are going crazy and start doing things that are out of character for you. All the things you said you would never do, you find yourself doing and justifying your reasons for doing them. If anyone were to know half the things you were doing or saying, he or she would definitely identify you as crazy. I mean, so crazy that some might even think that you're suffering from a nervous breakdown. One minute you hate him, wondering how he could do this to you, and the next you're texting him, telling him you love him and that you want to work it out, and then if you get no response, you're back to saying he's a joke.

Then you tell yourself you need to focus on you, right? You need to get realigned with who you once were. Like, who does he think he is? How could he end the relationship when you're the one who had every reason to end it? Why didn't you end it? Why didn't you say something? How did he get control over this relationship? And then the game playing starts. Those accidental late-night texts. The things you say at night that you wouldn't say in the clear light of day. This is the period when you're trying to feel him out. You start writing your thesis on iMessenger. You want to find ways to see him, so you communicate with him on social media. You try calling and messaging him and get nothing. Not one response. So this just amps you up even more. Who is he not to respond to you? All these years? All the things you did for him. Everything he said to you. So now you're stalking him on social media, checking out what his friends and family are posting to see if he's having a good time. You're wondering if he's feeling it like you are. And of course, you find nothing to tell you how he's really doing. You just find more reasons to get mad.

As if all that weren't enough, you start wanting to take the blame for the breakup. You start saying things like: "Well, I shouldn't have acted that way. I could have done this better. Yeah, I was wrong for doing that." And then, of course, you feel even more alone and learn that you just have to go through the pain. Nothing is going to make this better, nothing but time and prayer. Some days you're able to get excited about your future, and other days, you can barely make it. Your heart is broken, and now it needs your spirit and mind to help it heal. You have two options: Either you can do nothing and continue to feel this way, or you can move forward, expecting a much brighter future.

Yes, from time to time, you may have relationship flashbacks, and you may have deep heartbreak scars, but those scars just mean you survived, that you know what heartbreak feels like. These scars, and your memories, good and bad, serve to redefine your character and create a much stronger version of you.

When Will This Ever End?

After a breakup, you might wonder if you'll ever feel like yourself again. You're getting sick of all the ups and downs! It has to end, right? Well, for most of us, it's a process. I mean, you can't just turn on and off your emotions like a light switch. A very few people are able to move forward without much pain, but they still had to go through the process. Maybe it just seemed easier, because they went through the process while they still had the title of being in a relationship. Perhaps you've broken up with your partner mentally and spiritually but not physically, so on the outside it may look as if you're having an easier time moving forward, but the truth is, you did your suffering while you were still with him.

You keep thinking that with each breakup it will get easier, but it doesn't. As long as you opened yourself up emotionally while you were in the relationship, the heartbreak will be there. Though the darkness of the pain can't seem to go by fast enough, the truth is, the light at the end of the tunnel is actually closer than you think.

How soon you see that light depends on whether you resist moving forward or accept what is happening. If you truly love someone, in the purest sense of the word, you will never stop loving him. You just understand and believe that you deserve better, and just because you love someone doesn't mean you are meant to be with him. Your time in each other's lives has come to an end. The next chapter of your life does not involve him. In fact, you can't get to the next chapter while still being focused on him. And vice versa — he can't grow as a person with you. You may want to believe that he can, but right now, he cannot. Sometimes, in order for you to evolve, you need to leave certain things and people behind, and it just so happens that he is one of those people who can no longer have a front-row seat in your life.

Your process needs you to accept that it will take time and prayer. Along the way you will be detoxified; you will be purified by going through all these challenges. You must resist doing certain things, going to certain places, and reacting to certain things you hear. Your mountain to climb comes with a few bumps, rocky paths, snakes, and more, but reaching the top comes with victory and a great perspective. You will have some cloudy days, but eventually all will be clear again.

Any indecisiveness that you had about your relationship will now be replaced by some definitive truths. You will form your own new reality. In this period of detox (more about that later), you will learn to let go of anger, resentment, negative thoughts, self-doubt, and all the things you cannot control. You need to grow stronger, so it's time to give your emotional muscle, as well as your spirit, a good workout. Your belief in love, which you may feel is slipping away, is actually being tested. You'll probably play Beyoncé's recording of "Me, Myself, and I" a thousand times, and that's okay. Right now, it's about you. It's about reconnecting with God and with yourself.

While you know that this is not the end of your life, the pain sure makes it feel that way sometimes. You just have to take it one moment at a time, one hour at a time, and one day at a time. During this time you'll realize you've given so much of yourself to get a love you never really had and that it's time to reroute your energy.

You can't put a deadline on your healing, but you must decide that you're going to move forward. Anytime you feel an emotion, just embrace it. You are allowed to feel angry, hurt, crazy, and more. The key is to not act on these feelings, which I'll discuss in more detail below. Acknowledge that you feel a certain way rather than putting it to the side or resisting your feelings. Resistance only causes you more pain and delays your healing. This is your time to be truthful with yourself. It is said that you can't cry over spilled milk, but right now, you can and you should.

Embracing your feelings doesn't mean not being responsible for your part in what happened; it just means that you are letting it all out. You are facing your feelings and yourself. You are not waiting for the other person to save you from your pain. You are dealing with it yourself. You know that the one who caused the pain cannot possibly heal you from the pain. Only you can do that. Your ex can only put a bandage over the wound, if you allow him to do so, and that will only be a temporary fix until you deal with the problem head-on.

Your process may end when you least expect it. One day you will wake up and realize that you're no longer entertaining the same old thoughts and that you no longer have the same feelings as you did right after the breakup. You'll just feel thankful for and energized by what's to come. It may even come as a surprise to you that your feelings are now tamed. You no longer seem to think or care about the relationship. In fact, you'll be able to say that the whole situation only made you better. You learned a few things about yourself, and now you are equipped to avoid some of the same mistakes. You can actually laugh at some of the choices you've made. You've become stronger and better, and all it took was time.

Roller Coasters Build Momentum in the Wrong Direction

Above I noted the importance of simply embracing all the feelings that come up — the good, the bad, and the ugly — instead of acting on them. You might be tempted to make poor decisions just to rid yourself of your pain, decisions based on your emotions. Simply put, you make decisions based on how you're feeling now rather than on what is best for you in the long run. All your logic tilts toward trying to justify why it's okay to do what you know in any other circumstance should be avoided. We will discuss this in more detail in chapter 4, but for now, here is a handy list of some of the many actions you should avoid — at all costs.

HOOKING UP. You know how this story goes. Hooking up with other guys just for the sake of hooking up is a big *no*. Doing it for revenge, especially when your ex probably doesn't even care, is immature and dangerous. *No hookups!* You will have to face not only the pain of your heartbreak but also the regret you'll feel the next day. It's just not worth it. The process of healing is all about cultivating self-worth, and giving a piece of yourself away to someone who barely knows you is not the way to do that.

OBSESSING OVER THE DETAILS. Another post-relationship pitfall is talking relentlessly about the details of your relationship with others and exaggerating each moment as if it were the most epic moment of your life. Your friends know everything. You are the Nancy Drew in your own relationship, trying to unravel the mystery of why and how it all happened. But you are only doing yourself a disservice by obsessing. Get over the details. The details no longer mean anything. They are only going to bring up unwanted feelings. No relationship is perfect, so thinking that everything had to go right for it to work is the wrong way to think. It does not matter if one plus two got you to three and then led to four, because none of that led to your relationship working. The details are not going to help you emerge from your emotional rut. They will just upset you, because the outcome is still the same. You are not going to get the answer to the question you've been wondering about from the details. You already know the answer. Don't let your curiosity stress you. Details only matter when it comes to self-improvement, and the truth is, in any real relationship filled with love and forgiveness, both partners are able to let go of obsessing over minutiae.

BEING SOMEONE OTHER THAN YOURSELF. Your mind could trick you into believing that you being you just wasn't good enough for him. Your personality and looks were just not what's "in" right now. This kind of thinking leads you nowhere. You should only ever consider making changes to your physical appearance or personality when you want to improve yourself for *you*. You must make yourself happy every day. There is nothing you can do on the outside to address the issues you have with yourself on the inside. You can get an amazing hairstyle, new clothes, a new car and house and still feel the way you do. You are just deflecting your attention from the real problem. Your actions should serve you, not him.

CALLING HIM. This is a big no-no. No phone calls allowed. There is nothing more to discuss. Do not even think of calling his family or friends. When you break up with him, you break up with his friends and family too. That's not to say that you should be rude, or that you can never talk and be cordial, but let's face it; you're calling to keep the connection intact. This is not going to help you let go. If you left something at his place or he left something at yours, consider it a loss. Don't make excuses just to communicate with him. Be firm with yourself. It gets better with time. If he calls you, you do not have to answer. No more flying across the room when the phone rings to see if it's him calling. He has nothing new to say. No more good-night texts. You no longer play that role in his life, and he should no longer play that role in yours. If you get a call from him late at night, then you already know what it's about. If you are co-parenting, this can be a little tricky, but if the breakup is fresh, use a third-party person, such as a judge or a mediator, to handle your differences.

ENGAGING IN ADDICTIVE BEHAVIORS. You cannot allow yourself to be susceptible to addictive behaviors, such as drinking, overeating, doing drugs, or sleeping excessively, just because you do not want to face this difficult time. You can't hide from this. Your hurt is not going anywhere and will travel with you everywhere you go until you deal with it. The bottle is not your best friend, and neither is food. Nor is smoking a healthy way to deal with the pain. There is no need to pick up a habit that can and will ruin you. If you won't face your pain, how will you face getting over an addictive behavior? Turn to God instead.

STAYING OVERLY DISTRACTED BY WORK. You thought you could just throw yourself into your job, right? Well, it's not necessarily a bad thing if your work is creative and allows you to express yourself. Unfortunately, many do not have this option. It's easy to hide behind work, since it is a "socially acceptable" distraction. Yet it's a distraction nonetheless. It doesn't help you deal with your decisions and your heartbreak. Your job just becomes an ally to the pain. You can let it fuel you but not overtake you so much that you never get to deal with *you*.

REBOUNDING. Deciding to be in a new committed relationship soon after a breakup could backfire on you. Do you really believe you are ready to be in another relationship? Are you jumping into the next one because you believe it will take your mind off your pain and your ex? How will you ever know what you really need if you are always thinking about the next man? Getting into a new relationship too soon is not fair to you or to your new partner. Can you honestly say you are going to give it a fair chance? That you won't compare the new relationship with your last? When will you give yourself your "you" time?

These behaviors are all ways to subdue the painful thoughts and feelings that are part of the healing process. The problem with these behaviors is that they delay your healing and even invite some unwanted situations down the road. Maybe you engage in these behaviors because you feel you don't know where things went wrong, why they couldn't be fixed, and so forth. But what you will soon learn is that there is always more than one reason for why the relationship didn't last. So instead of worrying about that, turn the focus to you.

3 A FEW MAYBES

Sixteen Reasons It Didn't Last

> *"When people who have been together a long time*
> *say that the romance is gone, what they're really saying*
> *is they've exhausted the possibility."*
>
> —**DARIUS LOVEHALL**, in *Love Jones*

The end of a relationship can be either devastating or liberating, but it's always what you need. It's like going to the doctor's office when you were a kid and having to get your vaccination shots. You didn't like it, but you needed to get those shots so that you would be protected later on. Often we feel a need to pinpoint exactly why a relationship ended when it did and the "real" reason it didn't work out. The truth is, there are numerous reasons why your relationships may not have worked out (whether on your end or his), including a few universal ones. These are notorious for being the true cause of a relationship's demise.

Maybe he ended the relationship because he said he needed to move forward or needed some time. After a few incidents, maybe he doesn't trust you or believe that you fit into his world. Now let's switch it. Maybe you ended it because you were tired of his lies, you were never really into him, you couldn't deal with his lack of support, or he just wasn't "man" enough for you. See what happened there? A whole lot of maybes. There were more maybes than certainty in the relationship.

You may have been certain about what you wanted, and he may have been sure of what he thought he needed, but that doesn't make the two of you equally yoked. When you both see and understand your maybes, you can decide to let go of the relationship or to mend it in the best way you both know how. Or maybe you start trying to keep it together for fear of loss and of being alone. You step into dangerous territory when you try to keep it together on your own due to fear, since this can lead you to make some irrational lifelong decisions about someone who was only meant to be temporary. Now is the time to widen your perspective and to trust in yourself. When your maybes end up dismantling your relationship, you may try to figure out and pinpoint one major thing that was the cause and say to yourself, "Well, I could have or he could have dealt with the rest of the issues." But why deal with it? While no one is perfect, you don't have to put up with what you normally would have rejected.

The real reason many relationships don't last is that, at some point, someone checks out and never tries to check back in. One or both parties are no longer putting in the work needed to keep the relationship going. Four major things keep a relationship going: consistency, effort, love, and God. If any of these are missing from your relationship, it will at one point or another fall apart. Okay. Without further ado, here are sixteen universal reasons that many relationships don't last:

SELFISHNESS. Selfishness means looking out for oneself when in a relationship. A relationship is no longer an "I" but a "we" agreement, so when your partner is selfish, it is a trait of self-gratification. It's the belief that one's needs are more important than anyone else's. When your partner is all about "I" instead of "we," in due time this will cause problems. If one person is feeding the other, who is going to feed the one doing the feeding? Eventually that person will starve and will have no energy to do the feeding. The next logical step would be to go out looking for "food" somewhere else, and rightfully so. Here are some signs to watch out for.

He is selfish if he:

- always buys things for himself
- feels entitled to things without having to do anything
- doesn't make an effort to compromise
- makes promises he conveniently forgets to keep
- always wants you to call him but never calls you
- talks about himself and never asks about you
- believes his problems are the only things of concern
- wants you to listen and wants you to give emotional support but will not offer that back to you when you need it
- gives only to expect something back (if he gives at all)
- feels he can make mistakes but you can't, or it's a deal breaker
- thinks it's okay to manipulate people to achieve what he wants

- never goes out of his way for you because it's an inconvenience to him

If you've checked even a few of these, then you have a selfish partner. But what about you? Maybe some selfishness on your part caused your relationship to end. Maybe you like things to go your way, and when they don't, you throw fits. You may always see problems in your partner and not yourself, because you think you are too good for him, or he's not "good enough" for you (however you would word it). You believe that your actions should garner much more attention and credit than his because, let's face it, he doesn't do much, and what he does isn't that important. If that is the case, then it's time for some serious introspection.

Selfish acts are usually carried out with no apologies, and if an apology is given, that does not mean it won't happen again. A selfish person (whether it is you or your partner) is looking out for what is best for him or her. Selfish people never completely trust anyone, because they feel their happiness comes in making the best decision for themselves, at that moment, regardless of the consequences. The truth is that selfishness stems from wanting attention and believing that one is entitled to it. When selfish behaviors go on for too long, they will take a toll on the relationship and eventually cause it to end.

GROWING APART. The way you started the race is not necessarily the way you will end it. Your relationship started off great, but now things are *ehhh*. It's not that anything really bad happened. In fact, some really good changes may have taken place, such as a new job, a degree, a baby, a new perspective on life, new friends, money coming in...who knows. It could be anything, but you and your partner are just not there. You are no longer clicking. You have to force conversations. He is no longer the first person you tell your news to. When it comes to expressing how you feel and sharing anything about yourself or family, well, you keep those feelings to yourself. You no longer cuddle or hold hands, and there is a lack of intimacy. That one-on-one time no longer exists. You are no longer learning anything new about each other. You spend less and less time together, since it is no longer a priority for you or for him.

The two of you laugh less often, and the feeling of distance between you two leads to a lot more fighting than usual over issues big and small. Others start to notice that you are spending your nights out without each other more regularly. Your priorities may have changed and caused all talk of progressing together toward the future to come to a halt.

It happens. It doesn't make the pain of a breakup any easier, but growing apart can simply be about both parties going in different directions. In some cases, he feels like more of a friend than a romantic partner. Whether or not you were the one who drifted away, or you both did, you could not have stopped it, unless you both discussed it and made an effort to work on it. You may never know the reason he lost interest or why he changed, and vice versa. While he may know, the truth is that being in a relationship with you is not where he wants to be anymore. His perspective has changed (for better or worse), and so have his priorities. Drifting apart may hurt but it moves you into the space where you really need to be. Maybe you needed to get out of your comfort zone, or it is time for you to prepare yourself for the right man to come into your life. Trust that God has someone incredible in store for you. The guy it didn't work out with was probably supposed to be friend-zoned all along.

INSECURITY. Your mind can be your best friend or your worst enemy, depending on your relationship with it. With your thoughts alone, you can create fears and problems that can lead to possessiveness, neediness, dependence, and worries about things that may never happen. These thoughts may appear because of:

- external appearances
- your environment growing up
- current experience
- what happened in your past relationships
- incidents with your peers
- a yearning for love, an acknowledgment of only its lack

When you are insecure you can feel uncertain toward your partner and yourself and a real lack of inner peace. When one partner is filled with insecurity, he or she will display anxiety, nervousness, stress, and loss of trust. There may be signs of paranoia, suspicion, and lack of focus. When these things are present in one partner, it causes the other to pull away, distance him- or herself, and eventually end the relationship.

Perhaps your insecurities stem from a lie your partner told, which resulted in a lack of trust. I mean, if he is lying about that, what else is he lying about? These types of thoughts can cause you to suffer and will inevitably lead to a short-lived relationship. You will always question the other person, your relationship, and yourself. Insecurity can turn someone who was once interested in you completely off. It reveals a lack of self-confidence and can lead to erratic behavior. Some signs of insecurities are:

- always expecting the worst
- experiencing severe feelings of abandonment
- being overly inquisitive about the other's whereabouts
- needing to be together all the time because you feel he needs to be monitored (or he feels you do)

If either one of you feels as if the other has become too high-maintenance and can no longer bear the suspicion, the pessimism, and the feeling of being falsely accused, the relationship will end.

MATURITY. Lack of maturity can play a big role in the demise of a relationship. When one partner feels that the other has not had enough life experience or cannot relate or sympathize in certain situations, this can cause a rift in the relationship. Feelings of disharmony arise, and disagreements start to take place more often. When a problem arises, how is it handled? Are both parties able to sit down and discuss the issue maturely? If one person always reacts in a less-than-helpful way or continually speaks without consideration or has a one-sided point of view, this could eventually lead the other person to reconsider the relationship. Here are a few signs and symptoms of a lack of maturity:

- not being willing to "grow up" (not having goals or thinking about the future; not taking anything or anyone seriously)

- not knowing what he wants for himself (not being able and/or lacking the desire to handle responsibility)

While it is thought that age is the measure of an individual's maturity level, this is not necessarily true. Maturity comes with wisdom; one's ability to be open-minded, to understand different perspectives, to communicate effectively; past experiences, the gaining of formal and real-life education; and an ability to handle any situation in the best way possible.

Maturity on the part of both partners is a must in any healthy, loving relationship. It influences an individual's ability:

- to forgive
- to be supportive
- to wholeheartedly commit
- to take responsibility for his or her actions
- to effectively communicate verbally and nonverbally
- to work through any challenges faced in the relationship

If there is a lack of maturity in the relationship, one partner might interpret it as a lack of caring or appreciation, unbalanced priorities, or stubbornness. When your partner is consistently unable to be open and to compromise, or there are misplaced expectations, it becomes difficult to communicate openly with him, which eventually will lead to a lack of respect for him.

While gaining in maturity takes time and willingness on both your parts, you may just not have the time or energy to invest in someone who can't seem to get it, or you. There is a misalignment between two individuals who are trying to stand on common ground but are powerless to grow from there. If you have uttered the words "grow up," or have had those words said to you, then you know there is a problem in the relationship and it may be time to end it. None of us wants to feel as if we're raising our partner instead of growing with him or her.

FINDING OUR OWN WAY. Perhaps he needs space and time to find and understand himself and his path. His path may require him to travel alone, and it takes quite a bit of maturity to recognize this. While it may be hurtful to you as you try to understand why and where this has come from, recognize that this isn't personal but just a decision he made to better himself. Perhaps he feels he is "trying to be" rather than just "being." He cannot truly "be" until he understands who he is. You may have noticed some strange behavior or that he does not seem comfortable or settled in himself; perhaps he is trying to figure out some things that he can only do on his own. Whether these things are his future, un-dealt-with issues from the past, or figuring out who he is, the journey is his and his alone.

Maybe you feel you'd like to be there for him during his journey, but that is just an indication of your not wanting to let go. He is going to change, and you have no control over what he chooses as he searches for answers, stability, and certainty. Maybe he wants to get stronger in his faith, correct some wrongs, get better healthwise, or deal with any other areas of weakness that prevent him from feeling and doing his best. He may simply not be able to recognize who he is in a relationship.

UNREALISTIC EXPECTATIONS. Your ex may have had some unrealistic expectations about you. He may have thought you would wake up every day looking like Beyoncé or Kim Kardashian. He may even have thought you would be the one who cooked three meals a day every day while running a business and being involved in the community. Maybe he believed you and his family would get along, even though his sister continually lied about you and kept trying to interfere in your relationship. Or maybe you had expectations that he would be the supportive boyfriend — someone who would always say the right things, create an environment in which your friends and his would get close, understand your feelings, and always make you laugh. Maybe you assumed his family would love you on sight. Though these expectations may sound realistic, the truth is, your expectations are yours and yours alone and are not to be placed onto your partner.

Having unrealistic expectations of your partner can damage the relationship, since he may feel overly pressured and even begin to feel inadequate, and vice versa. Having realistic expectations in a relationship requires both partners to examine compatibility, shared values and goals, and commitment. Expectations from both partners should be based on wants, needs, environment, and circumstances. When you agree to rise to each other's expectations to promote growth, without jeopardizing who each of you is as an individual, then the expectations are no longer unrealistic but rather a sign of progress toward the common goal of uniting two lives.

The problem with having expectations in a relationship comes when one partner expects the other to rise to those expectations but does not feel the need to do so him- or herself, creating an unnecessary double standard. Unwanted feelings of insecurity and lack of self-acceptance can also arise when one partner is looking for more but unwilling or unable to provide what the other partner requests. If expectations were made clear at the beginning of the relationship but over time someone has fallen short and shows no signs of changing, this can cause tension and ultimately, if there is no solution, the dismantlement of the relationship.

LACK OF APPRECIATION. When you fail to show appreciation, your partner might feel taken advantage of. Whether it is over the big things or the everyday little things, a woman needs to be told that her efforts are appreciated, and a man needs to be told that his actions are noticed. Even when it's understood that some tasks are to be done by one partner, he or she still deserves to be appreciated. Showing appreciation is the easiest way to increase satisfaction and pleasure in a relationship. If your partner doesn't feel good about himself and what he's doing, he may stop believing in himself — and in you. You (or your partner) might feel the other person is self-absorbed, doesn't appreciate the sacrifices being made, and doesn't seem to care how much is done and why it's being done. These feelings can kill romance, and if the issue is never dealt with, they can kill a relationship.

There is nothing wrong with desiring gratitude from your partner. Your relationship should fuel you and inspire you to do and be great. When you are expected to do what may be considered "your job" (meaning play your role in your relationship) on a daily basis, with no acknowledgment of your contributions; when you feel as if you are not a priority; or when you find yourself asking for attention, you should either initiate a discussion about how to improve things or remove yourself from the relationship.

Being genuinely grateful, taking notice of one's partner daily, and striving to do or say what is best for that person is a practiced habit. It's all too easy to get comfortable with things being done for us and with having someone there to ease our emotional and physical loads. But when this complacency becomes a habit, it is only a matter of time before the relationship will start to break down.

ABUSE. Whether you have experienced physical, verbal, or emotional abuse, it is grounds for terminating the relationship. A relationship in which one person belittles, degrades, humiliates, or in any way harms the other will not survive. This is a dysfunctional relationship, and the abuser is in grave need of counseling and deep introspection. The one being abused must have enough strength to walk out. True self-love does not tolerate any sort of abuse that goes against the mind and spirit. You need to love yourself enough to step away and get help. You cannot help the abuser, nor do you have any control over that person's action or choices. The only control you have is over yourself. But by staying in an abusive relationship, you warp your self-perception and lose your ability to do anything for yourself. You may attempt to go to counseling together, and you may see some small improvements, but things will just go back to how they were. You are not the reason for the abusive behavior.

Abusive behavior is associated with unresolved issues and often deep anger over something that happened in the abuser's past. You are not the one who can change that. An abuser needs to consciously make the effort to change. This takes time and space. Your abuser cannot improve while in a dysfunctional relationship. Ending an abusive relationship is the most responsible action a person can take. This is for your safety and self-esteem, and if you have kids, for their safety and perception of a healthy relationship. If you have always attracted abusive men, then it's time to step away from relationship and examine your self-perception.

While many women stay in abusive relationships because they feel they have nowhere to go, no money, and no support, and because they fear being harmed, you must have enough faith in yourself to see a better life. You must know that great things can happen for you, regardless of what you have been through. There are support systems that nurture and uplift women who have been abused. Remember that abuse is *not* a sign of love and affection. It is *not* a sign of admiration. Abuse instills fear, a defeated attitude, and a sense of hopelessness. You will not be safe or happy in an abusive relationship. You will not be able to achieve any of your goals, and you will not be mentally healthy enough to make the best decisions and function daily. Many abusers will threaten you harm if you reveal them or try to leave them. The best way to get around this is to have a plan and get a support system that will help you escape.

BRINGING OUT THE WORST IN YOU. In any relationship, you look forward to expressing your love to your partner, growing, and becoming a better version of you. You believe your partner will be your best friend, your biggest cheerleader, your home away from home, and a source of strength when you need it. Unfortunately, not every relationship looks like this. Some relationships bring out the worst in an individual.

Your relationship might be bringing out the worst in you if you are always:

- upset
- yelling
- picking up bad habits
- no longer feeling like yourself
- distancing yourself from your family
- doing things you never thought you would do
- no longer seeking and growing your relationship with God (however you understand that)
- unable to express happy feelings and thoughts when you have them

Your partner, and your relationship, has brought out the worst in you if you find yourself always second-guessing yourself and making excuses for what's going on in your relationship and in yourself, to the point where you no longer recognize who you have become. When the person you thought would make you smile only makes you angry and the cons in the relationship far outweigh the pros, this is a toxic partnership that will eventually come to an end.

The wrong partner will be happy that you have given up on your goals if it suits his selfish needs. The wrong partner will humiliate you. The wrong partner will distort your perception of what's really going on in your relationship. The wrong partner will compete with you. The wrong partner will have you trying to prove yourself worthy to them. The wrong partner will have you acting out of the ordinary. One simple sign of this is language. If your way of communicating consists of foul language, and you started picking up the bad habit of cursing since being with him, this indicates that you argue in one of the unhealthiest ways and it may be a sign you are with the wrong partner. The right partner would help you feel excited about life and its endless possibilities. He would do what he can to help you achieve your goals. The right partner would do his best to please you. He would do his best to remove anything in your environment that stresses you, and he would make sure, to the best of his ability, that your needs are being met.

If your partner claims that you bring out the worst in him, you need to remove yourself from the equation. You may not be what's best for him, or it could just be him blaming you for his behavior.

Be careful, and know the difference between bringing out the worst in someone and abuse. If you're not sure if you are being abused, be sure to seek an abuse counselor. Not every relationship brings out the best in a person, but no healthy relationship brings out the worst in you. You can have completely different personalities, but if you can't be yourself or comfortable in your own skin and live in peace with your partner, then chances are it will not work.

NAGGING AND JEALOUSY. One of the biggest reasons that relationships come to an end is constant nagging and jealousy, which all too often go hand in hand. Constant nagging can make your partner feel as if you do not believe in him to get things together or to do better. It can also cause him to feel disengaged in the relationship. Nagging is not just something done by women...men often nag as well. People often nag when they feel they are not getting enough attention. So when nagging is present in a relationship, about 80 percent of the time jealousy will be as well. Being jealous of how he spends his time, who he spends his time with, and what he does and doesn't do, and comparing others' relationships to yours can also cause your partner to become disengaged, feel as if he can do nothing right, and withdraw completely. While you are demanding that he do and say certain things, your partner could choose to put himself in a space of isolation. Don't get me wrong; while there is nothing intrinsically wrong with seeking answers and expressing certain needs and wants in the relationship, there is a way to go about doing that. If you are jealous of someone else's relationship and looking at what you don't have in yours — and constantly nagging about it — then he may decide to end the relationship. It's often best to take the time to appreciate what you do have.

Isolation is not an acceptable way to handle a situation and can be seen as a coward's way out, but it is an easy technique to turn to when you feel you are constantly getting scolded, lectured, accused, or criticized, so don't be surprised when he stays in his man cave and won't talk. Nagging and jealousy are driven by the past, and this means they can be controlled. Nagging and feeling jealous are not getting positive results and are leaving you stressed. You will never have complete control over what another person does or doesn't do.

When you decide to stop nagging and to let go of being jealous, you might be surprised at the response you receive. When you allow your partner to do something of his own free will or to open up on his own, his actions will feel a bit more liberating. He did it because he wanted to, not because you forced him to. When someone is no longer criticized daily for what he does, he may actually step up and ask for help in getting things done or in addressing an issue. In a mature relationship, these behaviors and feelings should be directly addressed, and both partners should make an effort to ease each other's feelings and get back to being a functional unit. If that is not happening, then it is time to kindly escort yourself out of the relationship.

MONEY. *The love of money is the root of all evil* (1 Timothy 6:10). Not having enough money to do certain things, not agreeing on how money should be spent, and not managing money well are all reasons many relationships come to an end. One partner may make a significant amount of money compared to the other and want to engage in activities that the other partner cannot afford. One partner may be a dreamer when it comes to money, and the other may be more realistic. One partner may be frugal with money, while the other may feel that money should be used to live it up. When two individuals have different money beliefs that neither is willing to give up, problems are bound to appear. If a partner is not honest about his or her finances and spending habits, this will undoubtedly cause arguments.

If one person is willing to put his all into the relationship in terms of money and the other person is holding back, then feelings of distrust and uncertainty will arise, not only when it comes to dealing with money but with other aspects within the relationship as well. You may not have told your partner that you opened a Victoria's Secret credit card, or your partner may not have told you he spent half his paycheck to buy a big-screen television. With secrets come lies. If your partner asks you for money to cover a few bills, and you ask why and get a lie for an answer, this deception will cause you to change your view of your partner and the relationship.

When your partner lives beyond his means or lends money to individuals by borrowing from you or lies about his source of income as well as how he spends his money, this can cause an emotional, mental, and physical disconnect within the relationship. When one person is not transparent about finances, then it will be difficult for the other to feel comfortable disclosing information about finances to him. Money issues can be a relationship killer if one or both parties display greed, are not honest with each other, and are not in agreement when it comes to financial goals. If one partner is selfish and spends and manages money with only himself in mind, then eventually he will find himself single.

LONG-DISTANCE ARRANGEMENTS. For many, depending on the stage you were in when you began the arrangement, long-distance relationships just do not last. If the foundation of a relationship is not strong enough to support a long-distance romance, then it is only a matter of time before the relationship will come to an end. In a long-distance relationship, both individuals must be willing to put in the extra effort to make it work. You need to do more than just talk over the phone; you need to make the time to take trips to see each other, plan to enjoy special events and holidays together, and surprise each other with love gestures. Long-distance relationships test your willingness to work on loving each other and serve to filter what is necessary to keep your relationship working.

When a long-distance relationship is not being catered to or is not a top priority for either partner, symptoms will start to appear. The calls and texts will be less frequent. The conversations will be much shorter and may be one-sided and even feel a bit forced. You no longer take an interest in each other's days. You no longer make visiting each other a priority, and you make excuses about why you're not spending as much time together as usual. When conversations about the future of your relationship have stopped, and you feel the relationship is at a standstill or moving backward, then in due time, if both parties do not choose to rectify the situation, the relationship will end.

While long-distance relationships can and have worked for many, the odds are against a couple with unresolved issues, since the distance between you will not mask these issues. If the relationship has to remain long-distance for an indefinite amount of time, then both partners must be okay with the idea that the other will spend a lot of time socializing with other people and will have to adjust their schedules if they are in different time zones. Both must promise to keep a real connection going. It is all too easy to make empty promises about how you both intend to care for the relationship, but you must have an end plan, because long-distance relationships cannot survive forever. With a plan in sight, it is much easier to hold on and reach your goals together.

NOT GETTING ALONG WITH FAMILY AND FRIENDS. Your relationship with your partner will fall apart if there is war between you and his family. It's very important that you try your best to get along with your partner's family. While trying your best does not mean sacrificing your peace of mind and sanity, it does mean making some adjustments to get along with different personalities, whether it's his immediate family or his kids (if he has them). It's also possible that he doesn't get along with your family, and if so, you may not want to continue in the relationship. While the idea is to grow together and move toward marriage (if you're not already in one), keep in mind that you are married to his family as well. If you feel that his family has too much input in your relationship, or he doesn't stand up to certain members of his family, then this could be a deal breaker for you. More often than not, relationships start to falter when one party does not stand up and protect his partner against his family, leaving her to feel abandoned and to fend for herself. Maybe he has a child or children with a woman from a previous relationship; if all you've witnessed (and maybe you've even had to be a part of) is drama, then this may not be the relationship for you.

If every time you see his family there is some sort of drama or quarreling going on, or you are always being criticized and made to feel you're not good enough for him, then you might have to ask yourself if you can continue to put up with this kind of treatment. Could both your families come together and enjoy each other? Would it be sensible for you to ask not to spend time with his family? Would you feel left out?

And what about friends? What if you do not get along with his friends, and he does not get along with yours? If every one of your friends and family members told you he is not the one for you, would you take precautions? While other people's thoughts should not dictate your decisions, you must be able to look into why the people close to you do not care for him. Using discernment, you would need to find out where each person who does not approve of your union is coming from. This doesn't mean that your relationship will not last, but it also doesn't mean that it will. While you can't expect every single person on the planet to love and respect each other, still, you must take a hard look at the core disagreements and reasons for another's disapproval.

SPIRITUALITY. A relationship may come to an end when neither party is able to understand each other and accept each other's faith. There are plenty of successful relationships between individuals with different spiritual beliefs. While having spiritual beliefs may not be important for some, it may be a top priority for you. If you believe in the Trinity, for example, and your partner does not, this could be a deal breaker for you. It could be a deal breaker if your partner takes a very light approach toward spirituality, while you put spirituality first. Relationships do not work when one partner is always chastising the other about his or her spiritual beliefs. You may have a problem with your partner always taking credit for what you know God has done in your life. You may have a problem when your partner questions everything you said God is doing, and he just calls it luck. Maybe you are a bit of a traditionalist in the sense that you love going to church, partaking in certain church activities, tithing, fasting, and more, and your partner scoffs at it all. Maybe he is not into doing all those things but has a relationship with God nonetheless. Maybe you are not into going to church and taking part in all the activities, but your partner is. You must ask yourself if you are okay with this. Do you judge him for this, and if so how will this affect your future together, your walk with God, and your ability to be who you see yourself becoming?

If your romantic relationship is costing you your spiritual relationship, then perhaps it's time to end the relationship as soon as possible. If your relationship with God comes first, regardless of where you are in life, then no one should be able to destroy, interrupt, or question your relationship with the Most High. If your relationship with God is your fortress and where you get peace, then you need to protect this relationship. When you are able to keep your eyes on God, he will bring the divine one meant for you. If you can guard your relationship with God, then when the right partner comes to you, you will be able to protect your relationship with God, together as a unit, from outside forces. When you are in a relationship that shakes spiritual beliefs that have served you, you must ask yourself why you are aligning yourself with someone who may not be right for you. If everything seems right about your partner except his belief system, is that enough of a reason for you to let him go? Do you believe God can deliver to you someone just as fitting? If you are in a marriage and your partner has strayed from the spiritual path, it is better to continually pray for your partner's spirit rather than to nag him into doing a particular thing, such as going to church.

LACK OF LOVE. When you no longer feel in love with your partner, it may feel as if it's over. Relationships can end when there truly is not a single romantic flame left to burn. It can feel like your partner is more like a brother than a romantic interest. Perhaps so much has happened that you no longer respect your partner or view him as someone you want to be in a relationship with. You may simply have realized that though you love your partner, he is not the one for you. Nothing bad has happened, but you must let go of the relationship so that you're ready to receive the love that is custom-designed for you and can grow into another level of happiness and God's goodness. Or maybe your partner decided to end the relationship with you. It might very well be that he no longer views you as "the one," or he may have realized that he loves you and always will but is not in love with you.

At this point you may notice him making plans for the future that don't involve you. Maybe he wants to do things alone while still trying to hold on and not hurt your feelings in the process of a breakup. He may even hold out the possibility of carrying on a relationship later in life, just not right now. From time to time, he may check up on you or even give you hope that the decision to end the relationship was rash, but the truth is, you wouldn't be going through this if he was genuinely in love with you. When you are in love with a person, or that person is in love with you, the last thing you would even consider is a breakup.

INFIDELITY. *Everything*, and I mean *everything*, comes to an end when someone steps outside the relationship in any way. The trust is gone. Loyalty is questioned. Insecurities arise, and your heart will never be the same. Cheating can change everything you thought about your partner and the relationship and can even damage (if you allow it) your self-perception. You can't stop a person from cheating. It is his bad decision and not yours. Most of us do not work for the FBI and can't try to uncover what someone is doing twenty-four hours a day, seven days a week. That is seriously too much time, energy, and stress. Being strong enough to let go of someone who has stepped out takes a lot of courage and self-respect. Maybe he already cheated on you, you decided to give the relationship another chance, and it happened again. This can destroy everything you feel about that person, even if you want to believe it will get better. You might show physical symptoms of your partner's infidelity, such as not being able to sleep or eat. Some mental symptoms could include depression, posttraumatic stress disorder, suicidal thoughts, and anxiety. For some, the thought that their partner could leave them for someone else is unbearable to process, especially if their ex does not display remorse or work to earn their trust. Then you can rest assured that if you took him back he would just do it again. While you may want to understand why he cheated, it was still wrong, no matter what the reasons were and regardless of whether it was a one-night stand or had been going on for a while.

Don't Fall for the Excuses

Many women tend to get caught up in the details of a betrayal — wanting to know who he cheated with, when it happened, where it happened, and how many times. None of this matters. He may have cheated with an ex, a coworker, or just someone random. However it happened, the deed was done, and the details don't make the act any less painful. However, they do display his lack of respect for you. Regardless of how he paints the picture, the act was done, and if he didn't cheat with that woman, he would have with another. All he needed was for the opportunity to present itself.

Discovering the infidelity might have been traumatic, especially if you had no idea, but you can also see it as a relief that God has revealed it to you at the right time. It's up to you to handle what you do with the information. If you find yourself snooping through phone bills, credit card statements, and so forth, this is an indication that something isn't right. No amount of control or manipulation will keep him from making bad decisions. He is a grown man with free will. You cannot stop him from doing what he wants, and you must know that in that moment, he wanted to do what he did. We all have choices, and he made his. You may tell yourself that the cheating is understandable — after all, there's been a lack of intimacy because of pregnancy or kids, you are in a long-distance relationship, you just took a short break (meaning just yesterday you guys took a break), you work different shifts so you hardly get to see each other, you recently gained (or lost) weight, you're going through a tough time. If you feel you can't trust your man around other women or to simply go out with friends, and you think about the possibility of him spending time with someone else, then these haunting thoughts may be reason enough to conclude the relationship. Many choose their physical, mental, and emotional health over trying to babysit an unapologetic partner.

If you were the one who cheated, your partner may view the act as unforgivable. Trust has been broken, and his perception of you has shifted. Your actions have caused feelings of inadequacy, heartbreak, anger, jealousy, and resentment. Unless there is true forgiveness on his part, and an undeniable effort on your part to regain trust, then the relationship will never be what it once was. While you may have messed up, you must be able to accept the consequences of your actions and focus on your internal healing. If you are truly remorseful, this is your prime time to get yourself together and decide this is not who you want to be. Infidelity is an act of dysfunction within a relationship; it is *not* normal or approved by God. Cheating is a selfish, narcissistic act that in some way is almost always tipped off to your partner, even if you thought you wouldn't be caught. Whether you did it to seek revenge for a behavior you felt was wrong or you didn't believe the relationship was headed in the desired direction, you need to come to grips with the fact that you have caused pain for someone you once strongly cared for. Examine your whys and look for better ways to deal with them, so that when you enter a new relationship, you will not have to go through this again.

What Responsible Love Looks Like

In the end, it all comes down to knowing how to love. If you can genuinely have a healthy relationship with yourself, your family, and your friends, then when you meet the right man, you will be able to show him love. You will not have control over how your partner feels and what he does, but you can rest easy knowing that your love is pure, absent of games, and more than good enough. Responsible love comes with being able to compromise without losing yourself, being able to forgive, and accepting your partner as is while at the same time being yourself. Being responsible in love also means knowing when to end a relationship, even though you continue to love the person, because you value and love yourself enough not to accept an unhealthy situation. Just because a relationship comes to an end doesn't mean your love or your ability to love is flawed. There must be room within you to accept that he was not the right one for you, regardless of how long your relationship lasted, how emotionally invested you were, or all the things you went through together.

OOPS, DID YOU ALMOST DO THAT?

Things Not to Do after a Breakup

Whether or not you wanted the relationship to end, there is no turning back now. The relationship ran its course. Maybe you understand why it came to an end, or maybe you have no idea. You may want revenge, you may still want answers, you may want him to care, you may want him to feel like you feel, you may want control over what has happened, or maybe you are just happy to get it completely over with. You may feel great today about the breakup and tomorrow regret what you said or how it ended. One minute, you may be with your girls and feel empowered, and within a few hours feel lonely and start entertaining thoughts of how it used to be with your ex (you know, those good memories and what they really meant if it ended like this).

In chapter 2 we discussed some of the things you should never do after a breakup. Now it's time to really delve into the kinds of behaviors that you must absolutely reject if you truly wish to move forward and heal. Let's face it, when you are heartbroken you do not make the best decisions, and the decisions you make now will affect the rest of your healing journey.

If you have already done a few of these no-nos, which we'll get to in a minute, you may feel regretful, ashamed, small, or obsessed, and you may justify these feelings because you are hurt. But you can still recover from doing these things and feeling this way by choosing to stop responding right *now*. Not tomorrow, or after so-and-so does this or that, but right now. By choosing not to respond and by truly dealing with your emotions, you are no longer giving the situation or your ex the power. You do not have to respond to your emotions every time you feel a certain way. You do not have to provoke some kind of situation to get a certain answer, since that will not change anything. You should not allow someone who is no longer in your life to make you react against your nature and who God has called you to be. The key has been handed back to you. Your ex should no longer have access to your emotions or choices.

So how do you get to a point where you are no longer allowing what your ex did or didn't do to control your actions right now? The answer to that is, it's a process. It is all about making the decision every moment to keep your thoughts on improving yourself rather than dealing with him mentally.

The Never, Ever, Ever, Ever, Ever, Ever Things to Do after a Breakup

In this process, you decide to keep your thoughts off of him and on yourself. And then there are the things you must decide never to do if you are going to make it out of this breakup healthy and in one piece.

JUST BEING FRIENDS. You are fooling yourself if you think you and your ex can instantly "just be friends." Why? C'mon, I know you know why. The breakup is still fresh. When I say fresh, I don't just mean from yesterday. Fresh ranges from a minute ago to seven years ago. You read that right. Seven years. That's my rule. It's like credit. After seven years, negative credit items can be dismissed. In the Bible, after seven years, debts are forgiven. Anything after seven years can be entertained for friendship, and even then, you might want to ask yourself what the real motivation is behind wanting to be friends. Why are you trying to convince yourself that being friends is okay? You must always remember that in a romantic relationship, when one person is no longer interested, that doesn't mean the other person feels the same way. If you agree to be friends, you may be holding on to the hope that someday he will change. While you may not realize this now, since you may feel that he is overall a good guy, staying in constant communication with him will not help you move forward. Truly ask yourself if you can treat him as you treat all your other male friends. Will he treat you and speak to you as he does his other female friends? If he proposes that you just be friends, this simply indicates that he still wants access to your life. It shows that he does not want to let go completely and may just want to keep you as a backup plan. Are you okay with that? Take a minute to evaluate whether being friends with your ex will help you heal from your breakup. More often than not, the answer is no.

GETTING REVENGE. The pain is unbearable. He was able to break it off without any real consequences. You probably believe that you are the only one truly hurting, and now you want revenge. Revenge can take many forms, from faking your happiness with another guy to keeping your ex away from his children. The temporary satisfaction you seek is just that…temporary. It doesn't solve anything. It is just a decision to function from a place of hurt rather than a place of healing. Your desire for revenge will not make him come back to you for the right reasons but will only cause him to resent you. It is a form of control. These are just hurtful, evil thoughts that are telling you this is what you want right now. In the long run, when you know where you stand with God, you will no longer entertain these thoughts. When you want to stop your pain, don't look to revenge as your answer.

COMMUNICATING THROUGH SOCIAL MEDIA. As tempted as you may be to reach out to him, write an essay about who he truly is, or check out how well or miserable he is, cease all forms of communication on social media. The best thing to do, if he will not leave you alone and attempts to contact you while you are trying to move on, is to block him from all your accounts. As harsh as this may sound, it's the best way to let him know that you are taking the breakup seriously. Even if he was the one to walk out of your life, removing his access to you, and yours to him, is the best way to move forward (that is, if you truly intend to move forward). Stopping communication through social media also means that you will no longer communicate with his family or friends to get an update on him. This rule is a bit different if you are co-parenting, of course. In general, though, if you are not friends or were never in constant communication with his family, now is not the time to start. You don't need an update on his life, nor does he need an update on yours.

EXAGGERATING ON SOCIAL MEDIA. Even though you are in pain, that doesn't mean you want everyone to know that, especially not him. Maybe you try to come off as extra happy in your photos and videos on social media. You are now everywhere doing all these wonderful things, and you're leaving status updates and captions about how "happy" you are. If this isn't typically you, then why are you doing this now? Exaggerating about how well you are doing via social media is a quick way to demonstrate how badly you are actually taking the breakup. It shows how thirsty you are for attention and how much you truly want to hurt your ex. If you are thinking this is not about him but about you, then think again, because you know the potential of those still connected to your ex to pass along your new "great" life without him. If anything, this is the time to take a break from social media, since having other people's relationships on constant view can cause you to question why your relationship(s) did not work out. In the social media world, it's easy to think the grass is greener on everyone else's lawn than yours. Stay true to yourself, and know that this phase will pass. Engaging in social media antics will only make you a source of entertainment for others.

BEGGING FOR RECONCILIATION. Unless you were the one in the wrong and completely took what you had for granted, then begging for reconciliation is a violation of your self-perception. This isn't about pride or ego but about questioning why you are the one begging. If the relationship wasn't working out while you were in it, why are you acting as if you can't live without it now? There is never a reason to beg for what already belongs to you. If you have loved at the highest level that you could possibly love at the time, then you did your best. Remember, not every relationship is with the person who is meant to be "the one." In fact, some relationships are meant to prepare you for the one God has for you. Trusting in what God has for you does not mean you are to beg for what God has taken you out of. It's a sign of insecurity and lack of trust for what's coming next.

SLEEPING TOGETHER. While this should go without saying, sleeping together is not going to help you break your connection with your ex. This act alone brings about confusion and drama, and it delays the inevitable, which is making a break and moving forward. You are lying to yourself if you believe that sleeping with your ex is safe. It is just convenient. Sleeping together will not bring back your relationship and will only hurt if he moves on before you do. You are doing this because of your emotional tie to him, and you are only strengthening this tie, which makes moving on even more unbearable for you to handle. You might try to convince yourself that it doesn't mean anything to you and that you could stop it at any time. The truth is, if you could stop, you would, which is all the more reason you should make every effort to resist the temptation before you even engage in this behavior.

BAD-MOUTHING YOUR EX. While breakups can make you feel as if you've lost a part of yourself, it's always good to take the high road and remain silent about the details of your relationship. As I keep saying, the details no longer matter now that it's over. When you decide to bad-mouth your ex, you are inviting people into your personal business. I mean, you did once have a relationship with this guy. Talking smack about him isn't going to alleviate your pain. In fact, as many of us know, there are always two sides to every story. When you criticize your ex and the things he did or didn't do, you are just pointing fingers without being accountable on your end. Putting him down is your way of making you feel good about yourself and diverting the attention away from how you contributed to the end of the relationship. How you speak about someone else is a direct reflection of you. The only way to deal with the crisis of breakup is to get to the root of your own inner issues. The ill words you speak about your ex will eventually get back to him. Be mature, and handle this period of your life with grace.

OVERSPENDING. Sometimes shopping can be a source of therapy, a way to cheer yourself up after going through a stressful period. When you spend excessively, however, it is usually to fill an emotional void. While taking vacations, eating out, and buying clothes may feel great, you do not want to have to figure out how to pay for everything you charged on your credit card once you become emotionally stable again. When the time comes, and you are feeling excited about what's next for you, the last thing you will want to do is deal with breakup expenses. This can draw you back into feelings of hopelessness and anger, and the all-around feeling that if it's not one problem, it's another.

FEELING HATRED. With everything you're thinking and going through after a breakup, it is all too easy to let yourself hate, even if you believe you don't have a drop of hatefulness in your body. But when you've been gravely disappointed by a breakup, you may start to share your life experiences with others in ways that are discouraging, which becomes your way of bringing up issues that you have not dealt with internally. When someone you know shares some good news with you, you may feel obligated to tell him or her the dangers of this good news or make sarcastic remarks about it. You may even advise him or her on how to go about handling a person or situation in a less-than-ideal way because of your built-up anger. While you may not see this, others around you do and may start limiting the information they share with you. You do not want to be that woman who is known as "the hater" because of the unfortunate things that have taken place in your life. The best way to avoid being hateful is simply to stay true to yourself and deal with your issues. If good news is happening all around you to other people, and you have nothing positive to say, keep it to yourself. While you may tell yourself that you are only trying to help others by forewarning them, the truth is, this behavior is a sign that you have some inner work to do.

BLAMING EVERYONE ELSE. The demise of a relationship is not due to anyone other than the two people who made up the relationship. Going around blaming his mother, his cousins, his sister, his ex, his friends, or his dog does nothing but confirm your attachment to your relationship. Your goal is to *let that go*. The blame game is one you are playing alone. Choose not to take part in this game at all and instead try to learn from what went wrong and grow from it. You need to take responsibility for the role you played in the relationship. You can't go around pointing fingers if your hands are dirty. Maybe you chose to continue a relationship you knew really needed to end. Maybe you picked a partner who had all the warning signs of being incapable of the type of relationship you wanted and you still entertained the idea. But just because you become accountable for your part in the relationship doesn't mean there weren't other factors involved in the relationship's end. It just means that you are choosing to evaluate your own actions and to move forward in making better decisions.

If you go around pointing the finger, then you will always attract relationships that enable you to continue pointing the finger, never truly seeing the pattern that keeps showing up in your relationships.

OVEREATING AND DRINKING IRRESPONSIBLY. You're feeling bad, so emotional eating becomes your way of dealing. It's okay to indulge in a few of your guilty pleasures. The problem with overeating for days or even weeks is that the excessiveness actually doesn't help you feel any better. Instead, it just temporarily numbs your feelings without your ever having to deal with what happened. Then you find yourself on the scale, twenty pounds heavier and feeling crummy about it. You'll also notice your spending on food is a bit out of control. While you may not worry now because you're too hurt to care, you will, once your bank statements show the amount of money you've been spending on food and on new clothes in larger sizes. There is no reason for you to feel bad and get heart disease over your ex. It will not make him care any more than he does now.

Drinking your pain away also won't help. Turning to alcohol will only dig you a deeper, more depressing hole than you are already in. Alcohol is a depressant, so drinking will not bring you closer to feeling better. While it may look fun on television, remember that today's two hours of fun is tomorrow's twelve hours of a hangover, or worse. Don't let your drinking take control of your life, where not only do you lose your self-control but you also compromise your job, your health, and your relationships with family and friends. No one should ever have so much control over your feelings that you lose control over the direction of your life. Irresponsible drinking can lead you into making some terrible decisions that you cannot take back. How you feel right now should not dictate how your future is to look. Know your limits.

TALKING BADLY ABOUT YOUR EX WITH YOUR KIDS. Just because your relationship did not work doesn't make it okay to create a negative relationship between your ex and his children by bad-mouthing him. What happened between you and him is completely separate from how he chooses to show up and be a father to his child(ren). Your co-parenting situation will require maturity on your part. Try your best to keep your hurt and pain away from your children, since the things you do and say will influence how the children view and interact with their father. When you continually speak badly about your child's father to your child, you get into victim mode. You are most likely telling what happened from your point of view, which makes you the one who did no wrong (and if you really didn't, you probably wouldn't be talking about it to your child time and time again). Your child then senses this and may want to take responsibility for making you feel better, which in turn makes him or her the caretaker of your emotional well-being. Furthermore, when you choose to vent to your child about your ex, you might be inadvertently inviting the child to feel at fault for all your anger. As a result your child might start to feel angry at himself as he picks up on your anger, or he may constantly work hard to try to be what his father is not, always trying to prove to you who he is.

Your relationship with your child must stay separate from how horrible you feel about your ex as a partner or as a parent. Kids do not want to be around negative people and pettiness, and eventually they will not want to be around you. Regardless of what happened or is happening with your ex, teach your kids the right way to deal with hurt. They are watching everything you do and listening to everything you say.

COMMUNICATING WITH YOUR EX'S EX. Maybe throughout your relationship you've had to hear about your ex's ex. Your partner might have talked about how evil she was, why she hates you, and the many reasons they broke up. Maybe you got a few tidbits about her through his friends and family. Maybe you pity your ex's ex for the way she tries to get attention from him, or maybe you can't deal with her hatred for you. Maybe she is one of the many factors contributing to the end of your relationship. Now that your relationship is over, and you're still hung up on the details of what happened, you may be seeking answers from your ex's ex. The woman you may pity, fear, or despise is now the woman you are considering reaching out to in order to get answers.

And even if you feel perfectly neutral about her, this is still a bad idea. If you weren't friends before the relationship, there is no reason for you to communicate with her now. Yes, you would love to have someone with whom you could talk badly about him, compare stories, gather more info, and examine the similarities and differences in your relationships with him. It would probably make him mad to hear that you and his ex have teamed up to talk about him, and that may be just what you want. It may just make your heart sing to be able to confirm suspicions you may have had and figure out what was and wasn't a lie. But even after you get all this information and even after you've compared notes, it still doesn't change who he is and doesn't bring you any farther from your hurt. This is just your way of holding on to a dead relationship. If you plan to confront him with this new information, you may want to think about the desired outcome. Whatever it is, you are not going to get it from him. You are putting energy into a situation that does not want to be revived. If you want to move on, you cannot live in the past. By trying to befriend your ex's ex, you are simply knocking on doors that should stay shut so that you can heal. The only thing you are doing is hurting yourself with the stories and news revealed to you. By making an attempt to reach out to your ex's ex, you are resisting moving on with your life without him. Even if your ex's ex once tried to reach out to you, that still doesn't make it okay.

Be the mature woman who chooses to respect your past relationship and move on without the tricks and the game playing. Let God vindicate you with a better partner and a happier life without your ex.

BECOMING FRIENDS WITH HIS FRIENDS. One of the mottoes I live by is "When I break up with you, so do my family and friends." You know breakups aren't easy, and they usually entail you and your ex going in separate directions. But what about his friends? Well, if you weren't friends with your ex's friends while you were dating, why would you want to be friends with them now? The most obvious answer to this is that it's because you want to get under his skin.

Becoming friends with his friends is a very risky move. You just got out of one hurtful situation with your ex; why put yourself in a sticky situation with his friends? Doing this makes it uncomfortable not just for him but for his friends as well. Friends typically like to take sides and stay loyal to who they were originally friends with (which tends to be the one they have known the longest). Because your ex is the common denominator between you and his friends, if you are trying to make a clean break, becoming friends with his friends after a breakup can only lead to more drama and chaos. Take the time to examine your motives in wanting to befriend your ex's friends. Is this your way of staying present in his life? Do you want to hurt him? Any real friend of his will see what you are doing and will take your attempts as a joke, only making you look foolish. This is not the way to move on with your life, nor is it right to bring his friends into your drama with him. Whether you are looking for reconciliation or just snooping for information, trying to get it through his friends is not the right way to go and will only cause you more heartache.

When you choose to move forward and heal from what needs to be left in the past, you understand that none of these behaviors will help you do so. When you decide to choose *you* and to focus on your healing, you'll welcome in healthier relationships because you made sure your number-one priority is attending to you, while leaving the game playing and mistakes behind.

 SIGH — STARTING OVER

It takes a lot of courage to start over by getting to know others, but — and most important — it takes even more to start over by getting to know yourself. Sounds tough, but it's not impossible. It's time to change your perspective. Even though your relationship has ended, you are not really losing anything. In fact, you are regaining your sense of self. You get to take a new approach to enjoying the world. You have the opportunity to love in a different way. You can bring forward a new you, an upgraded you. It's time to start over.

Freedom through Forgiveness

The best way to start over is to gain inner peace, and that starts with forgiveness. Yup, the big *F*-word. Whatever happened in the past, whatever your ex (or exes) has done or not done, you need to be able to let it all go by forgiving. I know you're probably thinking, "Here is another person telling me to forgive when I'm not ready to do so." I understand, but let me tell you, your healing actually requires you to forgive. It requires you to say to yourself and to God that you are choosing to let go of the pain. You are choosing to take this weight of anger, hurt, disgust, and pain and release it forever.

You are the only one suffering. Anything that hurts or angers you is offending your spirit, and that is what is causing the unbearable pain. It is not in your spirit's nature to feel angry or upset, so to be in that state for too long is a disease of the spirit, and the mind. The cure is forgiveness. Forgiveness frees you. Forgiveness allows you to love again, and only through forgiveness can you truly understand your self-worth. When you forgive, you are saying that you are too valuable to be living in a state of chaos and torment. You realize you are a child of God with the ability to free yourself at any time. You are choosing to be free in his spirit rather than be bound by hate.

Forgiveness, however, is a process, like anything else. If you are in a place where one minute you feel like you have released all your cares, and the next minute you are angry… then you need to practice forgiveness daily until you have actually forgiven. To forgive daily, you need to let go of whatever is weighing you down about the person. Accept it as it is and decide that you'd rather wish him well each and every single day. Forgive yourself by accepting that every day is a new day to get it right. Forgive yourself by knowing what was a mistake in the past doesn't have to be a mistake in the future.

Forgive yourself by taking ownership of your mistakes and realizing they are part of growing into a better you. You need to give the hurt to God and ask him to transform it into peace.

Letting Go of Old Wounds and Baggage

The reality of starting over is that you have to be able to let go of old wounds and baggage. It's time to release the wounds that you never let heal, as well as the issues you picked up along the way that you have never dealt with and that no longer serve you. Let them all go. They are a disservice to you. You have to be willing to acknowledge these issues and to admit to yourself that you have been carrying them around with you for too long. Whether they are surface-level issues or deep down within you, it's time to deal with them. Whether they're communication issues, trust issues, self-image issues...it's time to face what you've hidden in the far dark corner. You are cleaning house from within, so *now* is the time to clean under the rugs. You are at a perfect place to do so.

This step may not feel good initially, but it does allow you to release what you no longer control and to close the chapters where bookmarks should never have been placed in the first place. You are taking care of you. You are addressing the issues you have been avoiding. You are finally laying to rest all those questions that may or may not get answers, but either way you are okay with it. You are owning your scars. You have the ability to truly regain your whole self. You are allowing all those old wounds to heal in the proper way. You are allowing your emotional baggage to propel you forward instead of letting it weigh you down. No longer can the things that once seemed so hurtful be used against you, since you see the blessing in them and can move forward in healing and love.

A Different Set of Standards: Stating the Nonnegotiables

Examining what's within will help you understand what attracts you to certain people and situations. What was it about a certain person that drew you in rather than told you to stay away? How were you feeling at that time in your life that led you to so easily open up to unwanted situations? Sometimes, when we're feeling vulnerable and are not in the right place of healing, we too readily open up and allow certain people into our lives. It's easy enough to do, but quite frankly it's the most effective way to harm your mind and spirit.

Perhaps you met someone at a time when you felt that you had no control, that you were losing everything. This person made you smile, intrigued you, and took your mind off what was going on. Everything seemed good, but he was a smoker, and you don't smoke. He was once abusive in a relationship (but says he has changed), and you had always promised yourself that you would never entertain someone who has no respect for women. However, you chose to overlook these things in the hopes that this time would be different. The temporary happiness you were feeling was better than the pain that feels too heavy to deal with. You do this not knowing that what you have invited into your life will turn out to be a problem for you in the long run, and maybe even a bigger one than what you're facing now. You are getting emotionally invested without even realizing it. This is what's known as the "creep-in." Your guard is down, and everything that makes you feel good for a while creeps in but then later causes some serious damage.

It's time to raise your standards again and to stand by them, regardless of how you are feeling. Standards are there to protect you. Think of it as quality control. The food you eat and the things you buy have to meet a set of standards before they can be sold to you, and then they have to meet your standards when you are deciding whether or not to buy them.

Standards are there for you to ensure that a person qualifies as someone for you to communicate with, commit to, and open yourself up to. Your standards are the entryway that everyone has to pass through before they can make an impact on you and an emotional connection with you. Let me pause here to add that there is a big difference between standards and preferences. A preference is not necessarily a deal breaker and is usually framed in terms of someone's physical attributes (as in, "I prefer blondes to redheads").

So the question you have to ask yourself now, based on what you've learned, is where your standards lie. How have you put them in place to protect you? Here are some examples of standards for your love partner to meet:

- He is goal oriented.
- He has a good reputation.
- He has healthy self-esteem.
- He sets high standards for himself.
- He is able to give constructive criticism.
- He doesn't see you as a burden.
- He is willing to do the work.

Let's take a look at these one by one.

HE IS GOAL ORIENTED. He is spiritually and mentally headed in a direction of improvement. He has a vision for himself and his future. He does not stop at or settle in his comfort zone. He is able to take heed of the direction that God told him to go, and he believes in what the Word says about him. Listen, if this man is willing to invest in himself, then more than likely, if he loves you, he will be willing to invest in you too.

HE HAS A GOOD REPUTATION. This may not seem important to many, but to those who value someone who takes pride in their name it means everything. You want to avoid womanizers and heartbreakers. Yes, people can change, but not everybody does. And don't think he is going to change just because of who you are. People change because they want to change, not because you made them. A good reputation among friends, acquaintances, and family is an important factor to consider when choosing a mate.

HE HAS HEALTHY SELF-ESTEEM. Level of self-esteem can determine many of your partner's behaviors, good and bad. A way to see where his self-esteem lies is to notice how he talks about himself and how he treats himself and those around him. A healthy dose of self-esteem is reflected on you. He can make you feel like the most beautiful woman in the world or be the one to tell you every minute how lucky you are to have him. A lack of self-esteem will manifest itself in insecurities, and it is up to you to figure out what you're willing to deal with. How he feels about himself will determine how he treats you and what role he, as a man, is able to play in your life.

HE SETS HIGH STANDARDS FOR HIMSELF. This may seem like it's the same as self-esteem, but it's not. Having high standards is an indication that he doesn't accept just anything. He is not desperate and wants quality in his life. This is his way of protecting himself. He has expectations, because he wants to live a certain way, and if he wants you, then to him you are exceptional.

HE IS ABLE TO GIVE CONSTRUCTIVE CRITICISM. You may be surprised to think of this as a must, but I promise you it is. You don't need a yes-man; you need a yes-and-no person. You need someone who will help you go to the next level. Let's face it; not everything you do is perfect, and if he knows how to give you constructive criticism, then he gets two thumbs up. He must know how to speak to you in a way that you can hear. This goes both ways. Can you give him constructive criticism? How does he react when you do? Is the maturity there?

HE DOESN'T SEE YOU AS A BURDEN. If you ask him to do something, he shouldn't act martyred about it. He should not make you feel as if you or any part of your life is a burden to him. If you would like him to attend an event with you, he should make the effort without acting as if it is too much for him. There is nothing about you that he would not want to make a part of his life, because it is also a part of you.

HE IS WILLING TO DO THE WORK. Everything requires effort. Do you get upset about what he "used to be like"? What you get in the beginning might continue, but it can also change, and often it does. What matters is that *both* parties are willing to put in the necessary effort to sustain the relationship, even if one or both of you have changed over time. When you make the effort to communicate with and understand each other, you behave as two individuals committed to a common purpose.

Being Progressive Requires Being Open-Minded

Starting over requires you to have an open mind about what comes next. It's easy to be strict in your thinking about what you want and just stick to that. When I say you should have an open mind, I mean you should still have standards but just be open to the package that your standards may come in.

For example, thinking that you have one "type" and one type only prevents you from meeting other kinds of individuals and exploring new facets of this vast world God has put you in. Also, if everyone knows you have a type, how will that work for you when they introduce you to all the tall blond musicians but neglect to introduce you to the short brown-haired stockbroker — who would be perfect for you? Again, it's okay to have standards and preferences, but you need to be open-minded enough for those standards to appear to you in the most divine way possible. Your type may have worked for you five years ago, but that does not mean it will work for you today. Actually, let's hope it doesn't, since you have probably evolved since that time.

Maybe right now you are wondering why we're talking about being open-minded when you're just trying to get yourself together. Being open-minded allows you to continue to be a student of life rather than saying you no longer want to be part of this aspect of life that God calls love. Being open-minded does not mean having your guard down. It means trying new things with discernment. It means exploring life and other elements of this world that you have yet to discover. When you are open to life's pleasures, you discover new parts of yourself and heighten your awareness of the beauty within and the beauty of everything that's around you. In turn, this radiant quality will attract the right people and situations to you.

Overthinking Ruins Things

Now that you are starting fresh, you might find yourself overthinking the many things that can simply just *be*. Overthinking can stem from fears and burdens that you have yet to let go of. Instead of letting go, we carry them with us and dwell on possibilities that may never happen. You can dwell on them so much that you miss out on the present moment and prevent what God has put his hand on. Because of all the thoughts running through your head, life is no longer an organic experience for you but a calculated process.

Overthinking can cause anxiety and even depression; you are choosing to think your way through a situation instead of letting God take care of it. This unwanted disease of overthinking can cause you to be your own worst enemy rather than your own best friend. Learn to take the moment as it is. Learn to love yourself as you are. Learn that what is to be for you will always be for you, regardless of what happens, so do not chase it away with your overthinking.

Overthinking is a form of self-sabotage. Your mind is trying to have control over the situation. You are not in a place of peace but a place of anticipation for either better or worse to come. The truth is, you block whatever blessing could be happening right in front of you when you imagine the moment to be happening differently, as if what is happening right now is not perfect enough. Simply cease overthinking by allowing yourself to accept that what you see is what it is. What you feel is what it is. What is happening is what it is. You move forward by going forward. Do not let your fears and past disappointments put you in a state of overthinking what is happening now. You are starting over, so it's time to let go of whatever holds you back from accepting more and better for yourself.

Just Kickin' It

While you are in this healing process, it is key to hang out with friends who are uplifting and amazing in their own right. These friends show you the beauty of who you are. They assist in your transition from heartbreak to healing. Your true friends will handle your heart with care and listen to you. Give yourself a healthy dose of exposure to those who want to see you in a better state.

As I stated earlier, what you should *not* do is hang out and be friends with your ex. Unless seven or more years have gone by and both of you have moved on, it is a giant no-no to be friends with your ex. If it was true love for you and him, and your connection is unbreakable, then there is no room for friendship at this time. Telling yourself that you can be friends is denial, pure and simple. It's your way of trying to keep him in your life, and vice versa. You are basically telling yourself that you cannot let go and, what's more, that you do not want to. Here's what happens when you try to be friends with your ex:

- It gives the person who wants to "be friends" the idea that there is a possibility of becoming more than friends again.
- Both of you end up living on memory lane and partaking in activities that you once stopped doing.
- It gives the one who did wrong an excuse to think that the offense(s) couldn't have been that bad...so no lesson learned.

You need time to breathe, and in the process of starting over, you must spend time with yourself and your friends. When you are slipping and acting in ways that are inappropriate or unlike you, your true friends will tell you. They do not want to see you at your worst and will do what they can to cheer you up during this phase.

Self-Doubt: Get Rid of It

One of the biggest obstacles to starting over is self-doubt. A section of your mind will try to tell you all the things you could have done to keep your relationship going. Your mind will whisper phrases like, "If only I had done that," "Maybe I didn't do enough of that," and "I know I was wrong for doing that." You may have all these thoughts about what you could have done to change things, but the truth is, it played out how it was supposed to play out. You may even have thoughts like, "Well, maybe I misinterpreted what was going on," "Maybe

I overreacted," or "I could have gotten over that." If it was supposed to work out, it would have worked out. This is an easy way to invite the wrong thoughts about yourself to take over your present and your future. When you doubt yourself, you are simply saying that you do not trust your decisions, that your instincts are wrong, and that you reacted irrationally.

You have to know that by doubting yourself you keep yourself stuck right where you are. You might even entertain the thoughts that maybe you shouldn't have broken up (if you were the one who ended it). Self-doubt will have you examine your past relationship over and over again rather than examining why you are doubting yourself.

When you doubt yourself you become the defense team for the issues in your relationship and you portray them as smaller than they really were. What lies in your self-doubt are your insecurities and lack of belief in your decisions and yourself. Whenever you doubt yourself, you are saying you are not good enough, and at this stage especially, you have to start believing that you are.

The Unveiling of Emotions: No Covering Up

"I have to tell him how I feel." The truth is, no you don't. He probably has a good idea of how you feel if you expressed it while in the relationship. If you didn't, now is not the time to do so. You are probably asking yourself, "Well, why is this section called 'No Covering Up' if you're saying I shouldn't tell him how I feel?"

What I mean here is not to cover it up from yourself and

from God. Stop thinking that everything is fine with you when it's not. Do not bury your feelings with other activities, such as work, without ever addressing your issues. You first have to learn how to be there for yourself. You need to be your own best friend. If you have to cry for hours or mourn the loss of your relationship for a while, then do so. If you have to write down your feelings, then do that too.

One of the many things I suggest you do, if you need to let it out and unburden yourself, is to record yourself talking to your ex about everything you feel (but of course not really communicating with him). Talk into the recorder, expressing everything, every emotion, without expecting an answer. It's your chance to talk without getting interrupted or being dismissed. If later you remember things you want to add, create a new recording. Let this be a one-day exercise. Do not revisit it. Once you have finished recording, examine how you feel, and delete the recording. Let it go. Think about the last thing you need and want to say to that person, and end it there. Now you can fully move on. If you are a writer, and writing works best for you, then write it down. Everything. Once you are done, burn the pages, or if you did the writing on your computer, delete the file, for good. What you have written is now done and gone. Give everything up to God. You have to let it all go. Ignored emotions fester and become problems in future relationships, since they also affect your self-esteem.

Right now is your time to let everything out. Anger, jealousy, hurt, confusion, disappointment, happiness, relief, and more…let it all out to God. Let God know how you are feeling. Give God the opportunity to make you feel better by giving it all to him. Be honest about how you feel and what you want to let go of.

Take the Time to Grieve

Grieving is a crucial part of starting over. You need time to mourn the loss of your relationship. Whether the relationship was great or awful, you need time to get used to being by yourself and doing things on your own. Give yourself the time you need to get used to the idea that he will no longer check in with you throughout the day and that maybe your Friday nights will have to be spent alone. You may have to get used to sleeping alone and eating alone and just enjoying your own company. Grieving doesn't mean that everyone around you will be grieving too, and it also doesn't mean that grieving should take forever. Yet you still need time to readjust to doing things differently. Whether it was a breakup you wanted or one you didn't foresee, the smallest actions you take throughout the day may really stand out now. Maybe you are a coffee drinker, and your ex was the one who made your coffee every morning. Good-morning texts no longer happen, and *Jeopardy* nights are over. Who is going to discuss politics with you? These are all adjustments that you'll have to make in getting settled into a new routine.

Finding Support

When you're starting over after a breakup, this is when you need your support system the most. Never underestimate the importance of your circle of friends, who are all there to lend an ear, give advice, and lead you toward a better path. Good friends know that starting over can be tough, but they are there to get you through it. You may not like it, but now it's through your friendships that you will be forced to get outside your comfort zone and face the world with a new pair of eyes. After all, God blessed you with friends with the ability to show you your full potential.

With family this can be a very tricky arena, especially if you have had someone say to you, "I told you he's not good for you" or "I saw this coming." No one wants to hear that, but in the end, family is there for you, regardless of any forewarnings they may have given you.

But here's the twist. After a while your support group will get tired of hearing all the details of your relationship or breakup over and over. They do not care about the why. Their main goal is to get you back on your feet, standing taller than before and feeling better. So while you may have their support, understand that your support group does not have all the answers and will need you to snap out of your funk eventually. You cannot and must not remain in this state forever.

Dealing with Ex Spots

Ex marks the spot. You know that certain table you and your ex always chose at your local Starbucks, or that pizzeria you went to every Friday night? If these spots are too painful for you to visit, then the simplest solution is to avoid them. It may be an inconvenience to you now, but once you're strong enough to break the emotional tie you have with certain places you can revisit them, creating new memories. Right now, some spots will always be "that" spot, and taking the chance of running into your ex or people who know about you and your ex may not be worth it. If you're not ready to answer certain questions with a short and polite reply, then visiting those spots may not be what's best for you.

Now that you are no longer in a relationship, it is time to do things differently. If you want to heal and prepare yourself for the best, what you used to do will no longer work. It's time to stop and distinguish between what you are doing because of him and what you are doing for *you*.

SO WHAT
HAPPENS NOW?

Where do you go from here? You deal with the pain. You start treating yourself well. You get enough sleep, you feed yourself even when you don't feel like eating, and you treat yourself to the things you may have felt deprived of in your relationship. You listen to some soothing music to get you through. These things sound simple enough, and you may think you're already doing them, but the truth is, the pain you are dealing with now is as much physical as it is emotional. In order to get better, you have to start caring for yourself and nourishing yourself with the love and attention that only you can give to yourself. If you hold yourself back from these simple but much-needed activities, you are only hindering the healing process. Take the time to get better.

You do not have to jump into any activity too soon. In fact, doing things before you are ready can make you feel worse. Be gentle with yourself. It's time to stop feeling sorry for yourself and to get into rebuilding your thoughts on who you are and what you believe in. It's time to start building your self-esteem. Here are some daily practices that will help you:

MEDITATING AND PRAYING. Take the time to speak to God about how you feel and what you want. Yes, he already knows, but if your relationship with him was suffering while you were in the relationship, then you must understand he wants that relationship with you. Through meditation and prayer, you will recover faster and heal your self-esteem.

TURNING OFF YOUR EGO. All the "I can'ts," "I won'ts," and "I'll nevers" are talk from the ego. The ego finds ways to protect itself and creates superficial boundaries that do not benefit you. Instead of serving you, these boundaries put you at risk of losing out on what you really want in your life. Your ego is not tied to your self-esteem. Your ego just builds walls to protect itself. Do not let your ego keep you from being a much more gratifying individual. If at any point you feel disappointed because of what you've allowed your ego to exclude you from, then realize that your ego is not working for you but against you.

THINKING ABOUT WHAT A HEALTHIER AND HAPPIER YOU LOOKS AND FEELS LIKE. What makes you happy and keeps you happy? What does a healthier version of you do? Think of what you want to dwell on in your mind. You'll give your self-esteem a boost at the thought of how all that you want is attainable. You can be the person who has the love you want, the career you desire, and more. What you believe about yourself can either boost your self-esteem or damage it. No one can do this but you.

EXPRESSING GRATITUDE. Giving thanks every day reminds you of how far you've come and the blessings that have been bestowed on you. It also increases feelings of self-worth.

THINKING ABOUT YOUR AMAZING QUALITIES AND ACCOMPLISHMENTS. Regardless of the mistakes you've made, what others believe about you, or what has been said about you in a negative light, know that you do have some pretty amazing qualities and have been blessed with some God-given skills and talents. Think about them. Live in those moments of accomplishment for a minute, and let them give you a self-esteem boost.

Learning to Value Yourself

With your self-esteem a bit bruised, you will need to cultivate some self-compassion. This is the time to handle your heart gently and to be your own best friend. You need yourself now more than ever. You can't expect others to understand or even care about what you went through. People have different perceptions of their world and yours. Not everyone is going to feel sorry for you, and nor do you want them to. You need to feed yourself with an overwhelming amount of love and care. Every thought you have must be handled with care. How you treat yourself and talk to yourself is extremely crucial to your recovery. What you say about yourself is what you believe, and your actions will follow suit. The energy you once devoted to someone else now needs to be directed to you.

In the process of repairing your feelings of self-worth, you will begin to gain insight into who exactly you have become and what you want. With each passing day, you will become wiser and stronger as you continue to tend to yourself. With every passing moment, you will grow your faith in God. It is during this time that you will gain inner integrity and a belief in your becoming. That tunnel that once seemed dark and endless will now start to reveal a bit of light as you make your way out and into your place of peace.

Now it's time to come to peace with and forgive yourself for any mistakes you've made. Each mistake you made was not to set you back or break you but to teach you and set you up for better things. In some sense, your mistakes serve as a wakeup call. It's not necessarily the mistakes you made that determine how you will fare post-breakup but the way you handle your downfalls and create an opportunity to do better. Will you take advantage of this opportunity?

One way we often fail to value ourselves is by holding on to a relationship not because it is truly what we want or because we believe that person will make us happy, but because we think that person is "good enough." You've gone through so much with this person and had such high hopes that, even when you know he is not the one, you may not want to accept that. Your connection to him was so strong, but not strong enough to keep the two of you in a healthy partnership, and you have come to embrace a dysfunctional relationship. But while it can be easy to hold on to something because of its potential and not because it makes you happy, at some point your spirit will choose to no longer reside in this place of dysfunction, and you will be left to deal with the reality of the situation.

You've Come So Far!

At this point in your journey you understand that your feelings are your truth and no one else's. You are creating a new environment for yourself that welcomes change. This new environment applauds your ability to let go and rewards you with knowledge, strength, courage, and confidence. You are able to shift what your day will look like and who you will welcome or reject. In this space, you do valuable soul searching and set parameters for yourself that ultimately create an inviting space for God to do his work within you. You have let go of your resistance. You have transformed yourself from a victim of hurt to an activist of peace within. You have now forgiven but not forgotten the feelings of being wronged, rejected, judged, and treated unfairly. You've given up living in that space, since you realized that you were the only one who resided there, and you no longer want to be trapped.

It's in the *now* that you will realize how far you've come. And maybe you are asking yourself, "What should I do now?" This question indicates that you want to move forward and overcome rather than wallow in what has happened. It's the past. You cannot go back to it, because you live in the present. You realize that you have control in your *right now*. It's in your *right now* that you can make the most of how you feel about you. Your present gives you the opportunity to nurture the parts of yourself that need the most attention. It's right now that you address your core issues and recognize how your mind, body, and spirit react to them. To be in tune with yourself, you must be in your present. Your body is not speaking from your past but is telling you what is hurting right now, what feels good right now, what needs attention right now, and where to go from here. Your past will never dictate how you should live in your right now without your consent.

Letting Down Walls

If you are now feeling hopeful about a future relationship, it is because you have lowered your walls enough to allow friendship into your life. It's now possible for someone to approach you, since you are no longer guarded or closed off. As your self-perception keeps improving, so will your opportunities and chances to meet other people. You have released the emotions that were holding you back.

Often we know we have our guard up but don't know how to get it down. And sometimes we're not even aware how closed off we've become. Even when you think you're ready for the next chapter, you become drenched in thoughts about why nothing is happening for you. This can cause you to overthink or to place blame rather than homing in on and identifying the problem so you can rectify it. You might find yourself thinking, "Well, maybe it's my weight" or "Is it because I have baggage?" or "Is it that I still live at home with my parents?" or "Could it be because I don't fit the accepted standards of beauty and don't come across as 'wifey' material?" These thoughts are powerful and dangerous, because they can shape your emotions and actions.

The truth is, when you become open, you learn to fully accept yourself. Once you've accepted and are grateful for who you are, opportunities and blessings start to pour in. You do not compare yourself to others or entertain what others think about you. If something does not agree with you spiritually and mentally, do not hesitate to get rid of it. You know where to seek counsel. You do not need to seek validation from friends and family for any decision you choose to make. With your new acceptance, you invite change into your life because you stand strong on who you are.

One of the simplest ways to tell if you're open is that when you walk down the street, people smile at you or say hi. If that no longer happens, it's probably not because people are having a bad day. It's an indication of the energy you are transmitting to others. Another test of your openness is your attitude and your conversations. If you went from speaking of possibility and prosperity to being fearful and storing up things out of self-protection, that is a sign that your mind-set is keeping you from inviting the positive into your life. Your attitude could be preventing new possibilities in love, robbing you of hope, and keeping you out of the miracle-prone zone. Being closed off means that you are still attached to something that is unwanted and uninvited. You have not let go, and it has grown more apparent to others by your behavior, by your indifference to yourself and others.

If you know you have an off-putting demeanor, it's never too late to free yourself. You can do this by putting yourself out there when you know it's time. By "putting yourself out there," I mean introducing yourself to what you were previously holding yourself back from. Whether you're interacting with certain people, going to events that require you to speak and look your best, or embracing a new way of living, you can overcome whatever thoughts and feelings that may be hindering your growth. It may feel uncomfortable and give you a bit of anxiety, but when you continually expose yourself to things that help you grow as an individual, you free yourself from your comfort zone and attract the right people and situations. By putting yourself out there, you come out of defense mode and start talking to people of all walks of life. Take the time to attend creative classes, such as cooking, painting, piano, pottery, and engage in other activities that expose you to people as well as cultivate your mind and attitude.

No-Negativity Zone

In your healing transition you must create a "no-negativity zone." This is the zone in which you no longer entertain gossip, thoughts of defeat, people who always say, "I can't" and "I'm stuck," those who complain or are ungrateful, and so on. You have just moved out of one negative "home," and you are not trying to move into another one just because it looks better. You are moving into a more spacious home in which your mind and spirit can roam in gratefulness, love, hope, joy, happiness, victory, and uplifting, empowering "I can" thoughts. You invite positive, make-it-happen people to this new home. Your no-negativity zone is crucial to your transition, since it can be all too easy to fall back into a state of feeling stuck, hopeless, and depressed.

Fill your newfound space with positive affirmations. Affirmations help transform your negative beliefs about yourself and your life into positive beliefs about you, the people in your life, and the inspiring actions you could take to propel yourself into a life of amazing accomplishments. Here are a few examples:

- I approve of myself.
- I am a gift to the world.
- I take pleasure in my solitude.
- I make the right choices every time.
- I trust myself.
- My actions create constant prosperity.
- I am a bright light to others.
- My life matters.
- I trust my intuition.
- Every situation works out for my highest good.
- Wonderful things happen to me every day.
- I forgive myself.
- My wisdom guides me in the right direction.
- I have the ability to make the best decisions for myself.
- I can receive all feedback with kindness.
- I love my family.
- My family is a gift.
- I am beautiful and smart.
- I choose to fully participate in my day.
- The work I do makes a positive difference in the lives of others.

Practicing gratitude is another way to quickly transition from a negative emotional state to a welcoming, peaceful one. Gratitude alone can help you recognize all the love in your life. You appreciate your journey and accept love from yourself and others. Gratitude helps you release all self-expectations and to express appreciation for all that is in your life. The more you practice the art of gratitude, the more positive emotions you'll feel and the more alive you'll become. You will be much more able to express kindness and compassion. To reap the benefits of expressing gratitude, take the time to journal every day about what you are grateful for. By doing this you are slowly changing the way you perceive and react to certain situations. Your focus becomes less aggressive. Gratitude gives you a chance to be excited about the changes you are making in your life right now. You begin to feel optimistic. A few examples of gratitude statements are:

- I am grateful for God's protection.
- I am grateful for my family.
- I am grateful that I have a source of income.
- I am grateful for the ability to forgive.
- I am grateful for the food in my fridge.
- I am grateful for my bills, which represent the fact that I can pay them.
- I am grateful for the hot water that helps me de-stress when I take a shower.
- I am grateful for the ability to wake up every day and make decisions on my own.
- I am grateful for my friends.
- I am grateful for being loved and forgiven by the Most High every day.

It doesn't stop there. In the spirit of gratitude, you learn about yourself all over again. Give credit to yourself for what you have overcome and what you are working your way toward. During this time you're able to put into words the love you have for yourself and your pride in your accomplishments. You can speak positively about yourself to others, or keep a journal where you write about all the progress you are making. Loving yourself is not about being conceited or selfish, or about seeing yourself as better than anyone else. But it is in the process of loving yourself that you are loving the creation of God and giving thanks. You are saying that the temple he created is enough, and you love the gift of life he presented you with. He thought of you and wanted you to become stronger in his image.

Loving yourself means loving the God within you. It includes loving the strengths, talents, and abilities God has blessed you with. He loved you enough to give them to you, so you must learn to love yourself enough to fulfill your purpose and generate the kind of love God wants for you. One of the best ways to start creating a newfound love is by writing down all the attributes you love about yourself. Every day, write down five things you like about your physical self, your spiritual self, and your emotional self. Each day, build on these lists. Read them over and over again, and give thanks to God for your attributes. This is a great way to build a solid self-image, while not letting the opinions of others dictate your thoughts about yourself. Whenever someone speaks to you in a demeaning way, and you let them influence how you feel about yourself, you run the risk of letting a new, negative self-belief take hold. So add to your lists daily, and ward off those negative thoughts. Here are a few examples:

WHAT I LOVE ABOUT MY PHYSICAL ATTRIBUTES

1. I love my eyes and how they shine when I smile.
2. I love my posture and how I command attention in a room.
3. I love the way my hair looks when I give it attention.
4. I love the way my skin glows in the sun.
5. I love the way my hips look in any dress I wear.

WHAT I LOVE ABOUT MY SPIRITUAL ATTRIBUTES

1. I love my relationship with God.
2. I love my meditation time.
3. I love growing in the Word every day.
4. I love my conversations with God.
5. I love listening to my two favorite pastors, who are supplements to the Word for me.

WHAT I LOVE ABOUT MY EMOTIONAL ATTRIBUTES

1. I love that I can allow myself to be vulnerable.
2. I love that I can still love even when I've been hurt.
3. I love knowing that I am blessed with compassion.
4. I love that I am passionate about the things I stand for.
5. I love knowing that in my pain, I can still do what is best for me and my family.

Seeing the Future

Now that you've made these lists and are feeling firm in all the things you love about yourself, it's time for you to create a new plan for your life. Where do you see your love life in the next year, the next five years, and the next ten years? What does a happy marriage look like for you? What does love look like to you? Whatever you think can become your reality. Whatever you ask of God with belief, he will answer. It's time for you to reevaluate what makes you happy in a relationship and what you believe would best serve you. You can now decide who you will accept into your life. What does your future love do that makes you happy? In what ways do you give love, and how well is it received? Use your imagination to create the love you desire, and think about it every day.

All too often those who are used to dysfunction continue to allow dysfunction into their relationships, because they do not know what a healthy relationship looks like. The best way to get out of dysfunction is not only to face your personal issues, as we've discussed, but also to envision yourself in a healthy, loving relationship. If you have never witnessed a healthy relationship, ask God to reveal one to you. Watch how people in healthy relationships treat each other, and take notes. While no relationship is perfect, this technique can help you envision what a happy relationship *could* look like.

While this process is about having a healthy, happy relationship, it's also about being able to accept and reciprocate love. You may not be used to having someone pay for your dinners, because you always dated someone who "cried broke." So when a gentleman enters your life, willing to do just that thing, you must know how to respond as a woman expecting love. If you have never been with someone who paid attention to your interests, when your future partner does, how will you react? Again, your imagination can create your reality. It's not just about what you want to give but also what you want to receive. Where do you want to be in your next relationship? From dating to marriage, what is it you believe you deserve?

By now you're used to hearing me talk about staying in the present moment. Everything is about what you think, feel, and do right now. You have already decided that you must move forward, but now you must decide that you want the best for yourself, and in order for that to happen, you must give yourself the best right now. You're probably asking how you can possibly give yourself the best when you do not have the money or you have no idea what "the best" would look like. Well, the best has nothing to do with money and everything to do with virtues that cannot be bought. The best refers to listening to yourself, giving yourself the kind of attention you would give to your closest loved one, praying continually, cooking the best meals for yourself, using your best silverware and china, and only taking in what feeds you physically, spiritually, and mentally. The best varies from the small details you tend to overlook, such as which plates you use, to the biggest things you can do right now, such as going back to school. It means putting yourself first and choosing to be around those people who challenge you to be your best rather than those who do not believe in your growth.

Right now you know what is right for you. With whatever external changes you are making, be sure you are doing them for you. Whether you are looking to rearrange your house, buy a puppy, or study Chinese, do these things because you want to do them. You do not have to make external changes if you don't want to. I do encourage change, since it helps to usher in new beginnings and supports your new habits and viewpoints, but understand the timing of the change and what it should represent for you. If the internal changes are not made first, your external changes will not affect your way of making decisions and of building a healthy relationship with yourself, God, and your next partner. Take the time to grow and build yourself before making these other changes in your life.

Some of the most effective changes you can make in your environment can be something as small as changing your wall color or as big as moving to another state or country. Here are a few examples of external changes that could help support your new direction:

- moving
- rearranging your home
- changing your daily routine
- changing your work area
- hanging out or shopping in a different location
- getting rid of gifts from a previous relationship

On Your Own You Venture Out

While you were in a relationship, you were a team, a duo… whether or not that duo was functional. You had a safety net for making some of your decisions. Now you are back to functioning as a solo go-getter in your quest to love yourself and to attract love into your life. But now that you're free to venture out and try new things, you hesitate and think twice about some of your choices.

This is your time to develop your decision-making skills when it comes to taking risks and understanding which decisions will advance you and your family. Knowing that you no longer have a safety net if you make a wrong decision should not limit you when it comes to partaking in activities, having truthful discussions, investing in yourself, and stepping out to do what you believe is meant for you. You'll need to be able to venture out on your own and be more than okay with that.

For some of you this may be an easy task, because your ex

was in some way holding you back and preventing you from moving forward. You could never take the risk of evolving into a more loving being, because your partner was too scared to venture out for himself. So doubt played a major role in your low self-esteem and your relationship with God, and it kept you from moving forward in your career and/or family. Or maybe your partner was the one who showed you that venturing out held rewards, and now, without him, you must be your own cheerleader and encourage yourself to do what your old self may have deemed "too time consuming," "not worth it," "scary," or "not for me."

7 GET IT TOGETHER

After God, you must love yourself first.
You must be able to love where you are and
where you are going to get to your place of happiness.

Everything comes full circle when you make it a priority to take care of yourself, when society would like you to believe you must take care of others first. But you cannot properly take care of others if you cannot first take care of yourself. If you are not in a healthy mental state, then how will you be able to teach, lead, and take care of the next person? If you are not spiritually well, how can you properly guide someone to God? This is why so many of us feel as if we are stuck and just running a rat race. We all must learn to take care of ourselves first. I suggest never making a single move until you have prayed or meditated first. This should be done as soon as you wake up. If you have a newborn, decide that you will wake up before your child. While I know it's easier said than done, you will definitely reap the benefits almost immediately when you attend to yourself before you attend to others.

What does it mean for you to attend to yourself first? Well, it means eating well, getting regular checkups, exercising, dressing well, engaging in hobbies that keep you mentally stimulated, and spending time with friends and family. Every day must be spent attending to your needs. Your body, mind, and spirit ask things of you every day and require your care so that they don't start to feel deprived and you don't start showing the symptoms. You need to give yourself attention in order to happily give others the attention, love, and friendship they need.

Eating Well and Loving Yourself More

Opening a can at dinnertime or grabbing fast food at lunchtime is not the same as healthful eating. Your body needs you to provide it with the nutrients it needs. Right now you're probably asking what this has to do with love and attracting love into your life. Well, *everything*. I can't stress that enough. Let's break this down.

As I've said over and over by now, you must love yourself, and the foods you put into your body are an indication of just how much you love yourself. Having french fries from time to time is not a crime against you and your body, but drinking a Coke every day is. Depriving yourself of the proper amount of water necessary to hydrate your body is another crime. Real love for yourself means only putting the best into your temple to help it operate at its optimal level. If you can nourish yourself properly, others will see that you are conscious of what goes in your body and will respect you for it. While you are not eating well to impress others, you are exhibiting that you love yourself and would provide the same type of love and nourishment to them.

Any man who sees you as a future wife will want to know how you plan on taking care of him (while cooking is often a shared responsibility, if you are the one who plans on taking on this responsibility, then how you eat is something that he will be interested in). He will want to know how you plan on feeding a future family, based on how important health is to you. He can see what you value based on what you eat. Again, it doesn't mean you need to eat veggies all day (while for some, it can mean that), but if he is considering you as a partner, then what you eat means a lot. How you care for yourself displays how you will care for him in the future. The same goes for him; if he loves to cook and plans to take responsibility for meals, then watch how he eats and tends to himself.

If you don't feel good about yourself, your choices about what goes in your body will reflect that. This in turn plays a role in who you attract in your life, since you're not only dulling yourself with food, but you're also guarding yourself against meeting someone who loves himself enough to take good care of himself.

Enhancing Your Physical Appearance

One of the many benefits of eating well is that it contributes to how well your body will serve you, including in the looks department. We all want to look our best, and what we put into our bodies impacts how well we look and feel. Certain foods, for example, help to clear skin and make hair shine. If you're wondering how this impacts your ability to attract love, think about it. Most of us are attracted to people who look their best. When you look good, you feel good, and you can expect good to enter your life.

Aging Gracefully

Aging doesn't have to be painful. Aging gracefully can and should be supported by your diet. One of the keys to looking as young as you feel (that is, if you feel young) is to eat right. Eating in a way that shows that you love yourself will reflect internally and externally as you mature. You want to be proud of every milestone you reach as you age. Below I've assembled a list of foods that are known to be anti-aging:

- yogurt
- chocolate
- spinach
- fish
- nuts
- avocados
- blueberries
- kale
- pomegranates

Cultivating a Clear Mind

Food has energetic power. Eating well and cleanly will give you a clear mind. Eating healthful foods and treating your body well can result in increased sensitivity, which means you emotionally show up in the now, with unclouded awareness.

You are able to show up in life and practice greater tolerance for yourself as your feelings arise. Those feelings of sluggishness, emptiness, or hopelessness can be controlled through a better diet. With a clear mind, you are able to be present and to notice what's around you. You are able to make better decisions and to stick to them, which not only benefits you but is an attractive trait to men wanting to be in a committed relationship.

Eating well plays a pivotal role in getting yourself together and loving yourself so that you are able to love others. It is vital that you eat the proper number of meals each day and that you drink the right amount of fluids so that your lungs and other organs can release the toxins in your body. Regardless of how you feel (and I know that breakups can lead to loss of appetite), you must be the one to feed your body and let it know that you love it. Feeding yourself well is a vital way of spiritually connecting to yourself.

Getting a Checkup

I know, they can be a pain, but those annual doctor visits are a must. You need to know your current state of health. If you have a medical condition, are you taking care of it? You must be able to put your health needs before anything else. You can spend a lifetime trying to fulfill a desire, but if your health is not in order, whatever you achieve will mean nothing to you, since you won't be able to enjoy it.

Choosing to sacrifice your health for a person, circumstance, or achievement slowly harms your body and your self-esteem. You need to make sure that you are not deficient in any vitamins and that all parts of your body are functioning as best they can. It is also imperative that you know your STD status — meaning whether you have something. Take care of you. Do not let fear control how much you choose to love yourself. Know where you stand, and go from there. If you maintain a positive attitude, pray, and keep God in mind at all times, all things foreign will flee from your body, because a home operating in the positive is not conducive to disease. Control your thoughts, and that will control what makes its home in your body.

Some of the annual checkups you should have are dental, vision, physical, and gynecological, including an annual breast exam. If your doctor recommends getting a mammogram or a colonoscopy, then get those things done too. The love you display for yourself by knowing where you are healthwise and by taking proper care to remedy anything that needs addressing helps you exude confidence and make better choices in your love life. When you begin dating, a man should be able to see that you are conscious of your health and take your body seriously, from what goes into it to how you care for it. When you start dating a guy whom you are considering part of your future, he too must learn how to take care of you when you're ill, and if you don't know how to do that for yourself, then how will your future partner know how? Neglecting your body is not an attractive trait to anyone. A man is going to want to know where you stand healthwise, and you will want to know where he stands. It may not be the most comfortable conversation, but if you want to attract a love that will last, it is a conversation in which "I don't know" is not a suitable answer.

Spiritual Checkups

The spirit also needs to be checked up on — every day. While no one talks about getting a spiritual checkup, you do need to be in tune with your spiritual needs. A spiritual checkup is not something that happens once every few months but several times daily. The checkup occurs when you wake up in the morning, before you go to bed, and throughout the day when decisions need to be made and challenges arise.

Your spiritual thirst is quenched when you spend time with God. You must remember that the solutions have arrived before the problem. Through reading the Bible, meditating, praying, worshipping, and inviting God to be a part of every aspect of your life, your spiritual self is in good working order and you can attract a man who sees what you stand for. You will not have to compromise your faith. Your faith will help you stand solid on taking care of your spiritual needs.

The right person for you will water your spiritual growth. If you are unable to get yourself spiritually right, it will show in the mistakes you make in the future. If your alignment with God and your purpose is off, then you will attract those who are also off within themselves.

A man who is serious about your being a part of his future will want to know where you stand spiritually. He will want to know who is leading you and how you seek counsel. He will want to know if you are someone who will pray for him and his family. Do you take prayer seriously? Is it a priority in your life? Most of us know that we cannot save someone who is not interested in the Word. We can only be an example of who the divine Christ is within us and that God will be the one to change his heart. You can lead a man, but you cannot make him do what he doesn't want to do.

Spiritual checkups are a valuable part of taking care of yourself. When you take care of yourself, you display the love and compassion you have for yourself and for others. When you are spiritually deprived, you cannot encourage your own beliefs, let alone those of others. Your conversations are always full of doubt and questions, and you resist God's truth by not operating in faith and instead only focusing on what's happening in front of us. Your relationship with God must be intact before you can have a healthy relationship with anyone else. Getting it together means getting your spirit in order.

Exercise Your Self-Love

It's time to take charge of your health. A healthy individual is glowing, confident, and energetic; makes better decisions; and operates with wisdom. And exercising the body, mind, and spirit is a great place to start. Let's look at some ways to do this.

Exercising the Body

Physical activity can improve your self-esteem and, of course, is a valuable part of loving yourself. Through exercising, not only are you saying that your mind, body, and spirit are important, but you are also saying that wherever you see room for improvement, you're on it. You are telling yourself that you do not give up on *you* and that you do not place your physical needs at the bottom of your to-do list. Through exercise, you can release stress, treat depression, and help your body produce the energy and stamina needed to make it through your day. You may also use exercise as a way to reach physical goals and to improve your appearance. When you meet a physical goal, your confidence skyrockets and you take pride in yourself and your ability to achieve whatever you desire. You feel so much better about yourself!

Simply going to the gym a few times a week or doing a few exercises at home will help elevate your self-image, as well as attract a lover who is interested in self-improvement. When you are interested in improving yourself, you are interested in improving the environment around you, and you are more conscious of what you would like to allow within your space. Here are a few physical activities that will help you feel great and will provide some mental and spiritual benefits as well:

- YOGA. Yoga helps you stay fit and brings awareness to your posture. You become more flexible and relaxed and learn how to handle stressful situations more skillfully. Through yoga, you strengthen your mind and body, you feel fit, and you gain awareness of your strengths and your limitations.

- PILATES. This exercise is all about body awareness and control. You strengthen your core. You learn to focus and achieve. The different poses guide you to a high level of self-confidence that will lead to feelings of empowerment, optimism, and determination. By challenging yourself with Pilates, you challenge the mind and increase self-awareness.

- KICKBOXING/BOXING. This is a great way to release negative emotions. You are in control of how you feel, and when you want to do something physical about it, you can choose to let go with an exercise such as kickboxing. This activity alleviates stress and frees you from whatever emotion is holding you captive. You are mentally beating away your problems for the day. You end up viewing yourself as a victorious individual, capable of overcoming any situation that comes your way.

- SWIMMING. This form of cardiovascular exercise helps you control your breathing, regardless of what is happening. You learn how to swim with and against the waves. This also helps you deal with situations that come up in your day and the way your body reacts to them. Swimming is a great way to release stress and to challenge the body and mind. It helps to establish a conqueror attitude in overcoming any obstacle, no matter what is going up against the body. It is also a great way to stay fit and to exercise many muscles in the body at the same time.

- RUNNING. Running will change your outlook on who you are and what you can accomplish. It will give you the confidence to defy mental and physical limits and help you to push yourself. If you are into running marathons, this is a unique way to release what you have been mentally holding on to, focus on the task at hand, and push yourself forward to a new goal. Every time you achieve one goal, you build the self-confidence to accomplish another.

Exercising the Mind

Exercising isn't just physical but mental as well. Doing mental exercises often, even daily, will help you face the tasks and challenges ahead. Here are a few mental exercises to get you going:

- STUDY A NEW LANGUAGE. This not only helps boost your brain power, but it also assists in your ability to multitask, improves memory, widens your perspective of the world and other peoples, sharpens your reading skills, and helps you express yourself, problem solve, and negotiate.

- CHALLENGE YOUR PALATE. Trying new foods, as well as trying to identify the ingredients in your food, is fun and helps to improve recognition and memory. You can also do this by testing your knowledge of wines as you wine-taste.

- DO THOSE MATH PROBLEMS IN YOUR HEAD. Step away from your phone or calculator and figure out that math problem with good old pencil, paper, and brains.

- TELL A STORY. Telling stories challenges your brain to focus on details and to tie an emotion to those details. Plus, it's great entertainment!

Exercising the Spirit

Along with physical and mental workouts, we also need spiritual ones to keep our faith in tip-top shape. Just like any muscle, if you don't use it, it becomes weak and ill-equipped for the job at hand. Here are some great spiritual exercises:

- PRACTICE BEING A GIVER. You can do this by tithing and devoting your time to helping someone else.

- IDENTIFY YOUR BLESSINGS. Identify your blessings, and be thankful for them.

- SHARE YOUR TESTIMONY. Tell your story to those willing to listen. You can help them with their journey as you share your testimony of how God has been great to you and has loved you along the way.

- FAST. Detox the body and the mind, and focus on what is private between you and God.

- SPEND TIME IN NATURE. Doing this allows you to feel spiritually connected to all living things and to understand the meaning of being one with God. Dwell in the beauty of your present and of all the gifts of the planet.

Self-Reflection: Dressing Well

"You sound like you're wearing sweatpants."

Dressing up should be fun. Most likely as a little girl you used to love to dress up in your mother's or sister's or grandmother's clothes, and to dress up your dolls as well. The idea was to look nice and pretend to be someone you admired or respected. As time passed, you either stepped up the attention you gave to your attire, or you barely gave yourself the time needed to put yourself together. The world can tell how you feel about yourself by the way you dress. You can argue this until you no longer have the energy to say another word, but the truth will always remain that how you dress is a direct reflection of how you feel about yourself.

When you dress with care and confidence, it's an external way of showing that you respect yourself. The daily attention you give to yourself displays that you always present your best self, even when you do not feel like it. When you look good, you feel good, and your actions line up with how you feel.

It's obvious to others when you wake up and throw on some clothes without really caring about what you're doing. You can guess what message that sends to those who come into contact with you, but more important, you can guess what message that sends to *you*. Every time you dress in a less than desirable way, you are saying to yourself, "This is who I am," "This is what I believe I deserve," and "This is as good as it gets on a typical day." How you wear your ensemble is a direct correlation to how you feel about yourself and the world around you. Your mind and spirit only make moves that they believe in. That's why the saying "Actions over words" holds so much truth.

Self-neglect can lead to feeling bad, looking bad, and acting indifferent, and this includes whether you give any attention to your sense of style and self. When you stop neglecting yourself on the outside, more than likely you will stop neglecting yourself on the inside as well. Getting compliments on how you look also encourages you to keep treating yourself better, to become more poised, and to go about your daily activities with self-assurance. Here are some things you can do to present yourself in the best light:

- Iron your clothes.
- Wear clothes that fit.

- Dry-clean what needs to be dry-cleaned.
- Put on your favorite seasonal perfume.
- Always arrive put together.
- Master your personal style.

First impressions are made instantly. Just by looking at how you wear your clothes, people make judgments, such as if you are approachable or are someone to avoid, if you are trustworthy, likable, and confident or someone who can be taken for granted. While these judgments may not be based on reality, they still affect how others treat you. In the process of loving yourself first and attracting love, you must pay special attention to details (especially those that help you feel more like yourself) so you can imbue your everyday actions with confidence and self-love.

Mentally Stimulating Hobbies

"My skin is glowing, my bank accounts are growing, and my relationship with God is better. Life is great. That's the goal."

It truly is great when you make the time to improve yourself. Establishing interests in certain areas of life, such as the arts, your community, your church, sports, and other extracurricular activities allows you to grow in terms of communication skills, emotional development, and the cultivation of new ways of thinking.

From taking a cooking class to visiting museums to gardening, it is time to take up some activities you truly enjoy. Staying in the house and doing the same routine hinders your ability to get over a bad situation and prevents the doors of growth from opening. The activities you choose should be of genuine interest to you. They should intrigue you in some way or be something you've always wanted to try.

If you have a list of activities that intrigue you, why not take the time to try one now? You do not need to be in a relationship to do something you've always wanted to do. You are still in good company when you do these activities with friends or family or *by yourself*. Learn to enjoy your own company. Defeat your fears and the thoughts in your head that say you can't do certain things alone. When you learn to take joy in your own company and be at peace and confident when engaging in new activities, you become unstoppable. It might help you to realize that though you don't *need* company to be happy, you may *want* company. There are several benefits to taking on a hobby and participating in new activities. I will list just a few of them. Taking on a new hobby:

- raises self-esteem
- diversifies your interests
- builds relationship skills
- exercises the ability to contribute

If there is an area you feel weak in, or you just want to explore an untapped talent, participating in an activity that helps you develop unexplored parts of yourself can increase your self-knowledge, create lasting memories, and build toward your self-perception. Many of us would love to excel at something, and especially as we get older, we would like to know that we can still sharpen our skills. Taking the time to expand your horizons and build your skill set is an investment well worth looking into.

Perhaps you need to improve your relationship skills, and if so, taking on new activities with all different kinds of people can help you do just that. Mixing what you love with what you are curious about is one of the best ways to diversify your interests. This diversification will allow you to meet new people, to have different conversations and perspectives. It allows you to appreciate your world on a much grander scale. Here are a few activities and hobbies that will help you do that:

- writing
- horseback riding
- singing lessons
- knitting
- gardening
- swimming
- calligraphy
- learning a new language
- sculpting
- interior design/renovation
- playing the violin
- any church activity that strikes your interest
- taking part in local theater productions
- taking a class to learn a skill such as Photoshop

It's in the openness of your heart as you try out new hobbies that you also discover what you are truly passionate about. You have given yourself the opportunity to interact with people who share your interests and passions. As such, you are able to express a part of yourself that may have taken a backseat due to stress or routine or people in your life holding you back. Making time for your activities allows you to put *you* first and to open yourself up to a potential love interest with the same interests. Although you engage in your activities for you, you also allow the wonderful possibility of love to find its way to you, often when you least expect it, when you express yourself through your creative outlets. Whether or not you are ready to open yourself up to love, you are healing just by having an outlet that allows you to create and to discover an aspect of yourself that you may have silenced or taken for granted.

If you are known to be predictable, now is the time to awaken your senses and step into the blessings and opportunities that God has offered to you. You are never too old or too young to live right now.

The Rediscovery of You

Part of why I stress the importance of learning where your passions lie is that in picking up the pieces to create a new and improved *you*, which I like to call version 2.0, you must first know who you are. You must know where you stand, where your boundaries lie, what you like, what makes you happy, who you are in any given environment, and more. I could go on and on, but ultimately the truth lies in knowing that what once was able to shake you cannot permanently break you. Even at your most vulnerable times, you know that you *can* and *will* get back up. Your feeling broken is not the same as being broken. You are not damaged. Your many times of hurt and pain expose your weak areas and give you the opportunity to strengthen them. Regardless of how things turned out in your past relationships, you have the opportunity to do and be better for yourself. You consciously state that your next man will not see you behaving as you once did, because you yourself did not like behaving like that. You also state that you will no longer allow anyone to make you feel less than.

You get what you believe. This rule applies to anything in life, but in this context, what you believe about yourself is what you will attract into your life. If you have ever wondered why certain people seem so confident that they always expect their word to be taken as the only truth, well, that comes from knowing and believing that they can be, have, and do whatever they want. They know who they are, whether or not others believe the things they profess. They are able to stand firm in their self-knowledge and have an unshakable self-esteem. They are not concerned with how others perceive them or whether they are accepted or understood by others. Rather, they know that they are enough as they are and that whatever is going on around them fits their world, and not the other way around.

You are the daughter of the Most High. You are a queen. You were created out of love. You are powerful and undeniably remarkable. You are a one-of-a-kind woman whose beauty radiates from her spirit and makes its way out to the world. You are a valuable, lovable, divinely made woman. You are needed, loved, and respected. Your presence is a blessing. Your gift is impressive, and you are here because you are needed. You have something to offer the world. There is no one like you. There will never be anyone like you. Your smile is needed. Your thoughts are needed. Your heart is needed. Your spirit is needed.

You are the miracle that someone prayed for. You are a blessing to others. You make a difference. You are the difference, because you are different. You are "that" woman. You are God's child. You are worthy. You are someone's reason to smile. You are appreciated. You are as important today as you were years ago. You have a place in this world.

Those words of affirmation reflect the truth of who you are. When you truly know this, then you can make decisions based on your beliefs about yourself. Your decisions serve not only you but also those around you.

It is in the rediscovery of who you are and who you always were in God that you understand your purpose. Instead of living behind who others want you to be or getting lost in an identity that is forced on you, you can choose to embrace the beauty of you.

When you choose to lead a life that is true to you, you attract people and situations that truly align with your values. You understand who and what you want in your life and stop worrying about what everyone else wants for you. You are able to uncover hidden truths and gain insights about you and your inner world.

When rediscovering who you are, you must get back to the basics, and one way to do that is to answer a few simple questions about yourself. It's also valuable to know the whys to each answer, to understand their meaning to you. Here are a few questions to ask yourself:

- What motivates me? Why?
- What's my favorite food? Why?

- What makes me happy? Why?
- What do I consider my greatest accomplishment? Why?
- What are my three biggest priorities right now? Why?
- If money were no object, what would I do all day? Why?
- How would I describe myself? Why?
- Aside from the necessities, what's one thing I could not go a day without? Why?
- What is my favorite color? Why?
- How do I handle tough situations? Why?
- What makes me smile? Why?
- Would I call myself an introvert or an extrovert? Why?
- Which of my five senses would I say is my strongest? Why?
- How well do I follow my instincts? Why?
- What is my personal motto? Why?
- What are the three things I think about almost every day? Why?
- What is my dream job? Why?
- What would I like to do on my own? Why?
- What would I like to do with a group of friends? Why?
- What is one thing I will never do again? Why?
- Who knows me best? Why?
- What would I like to do over and over again? Why?
- What would I like others to say about me? Why?
- What do I care about most? Why?

Putting Your Love on a Pedestal

In the effort to get to that place where you feel whole, you need to make a conscious decision that your love is enough not only for the right person but ultimately for you. If you were to receive the love that you give to others, would you be happy? I am asking this question because I believe you have a deep understanding of what love is and what it looks like:

> *Love is patient, love is kind. It does not envy, it does not boast, it is not proud. It does not dishonor others, it is not self-seeking, it is not easily angered, it keeps no record of wrongs. Love does not delight in evil but rejoices with the truth. It always protects, always trusts, always hopes, always perseveres.* (1 Corinthians 13:4–7, NIV)

On some level you know that your love is enough. Your love in the purest form displays truth, vulnerability, loyalty, compassion, joy, energy, and healing. The belief that you need more material things or that you need people to love you is false. When you understand the love in which God created you, the love that saved you, as well as your self-love, which doesn't seek validation from others, then you are truly in tune with yourself and can operate from a space of wholeness.

THESE THINGS NEED TO CHANGE

You've learned a few lessons. You may have figured out a few things about yourself that you don't like, and a few things you may feel you would do differently now. You may even begin to understand that you weren't perfect in your relationship, and although he was what you wanted, he was far from what you needed. Your mind and spirit are now making adjustments so they can function with clarity. It's not so much what you went through that matters but how you handled it and what you took away from it. If you truly feel like you made no mistakes and did nothing wrong, then this is really the time for self-examination. Some of your choices led you to pick that particular individual. You may not have done anything drastically damaging or even anything worth talking about, but you still needed to use discernment. You have to accept that he isn't the guy. No matter how much you want to fit that one piece into your world, it no longer belongs there. He doesn't truly want to be a part of your world, because if he did, his actions and words would consistently show his love for you, not just when he is in a good mood or wants something.

So things have to change. It's time to break down the walls of habit in thought and action. You must have a plan for what you want and need and the direction you plan on going in. With a concrete plan in hand, ask yourself if you already have all that you want and believe for yourself. If the answer is no, then it is time for change. If the answer is yes (and I want you to really think about this if you keep attracting the same type of men), then you need to raise your standards in regards to what you are expecting and accepting.

Now that you are in a new space, with a new set of feelings to fuel your thoughts, it's time to let go of the old thoughts that no longer serve you and refine those that are there to protect you. In the process of moving forward and letting go, you must reset your mind. Fighting against how you feel does not make change come about easily. In fact, it does the complete opposite. You use the little energy you have in trying to offset your pain, making it much more painful to heal and harder to create change for yourself.

Attitude and Outlook

"I've got a new attitude."

— "New Attitude," performed by **PATTI LABELLE**

One of the changes you will need to consider in stepping into your better self is to improve your attitude and outlook.

If there was ever a time you thought or uttered the phrase "Being single isn't that bad," guess what? You're right. It's not bad at all. The grass isn't always greener on the other side. It's greener wherever you water it.

So now you are single. You are in a space you may not have wanted to be in again, but hey, you're here, and it's time to grow the grass you stand on. Maybe you feel you function better when you are in a relationship, or you're someone who always needs to be in a relationship to feel justified or whole. Let's examine that. You are more than who you are in a relationship. Your opinions as an individual matter. Your decisions as an individual matter. You should not feel comfortable being defined only by your couplehood status. If you believe that you always need to be referred to as "Robert and his girl," then it's time for some introspection. Why do you feel you are not strong enough to stand on your own? Why is your attachment to him so strong that you lose your sense of self? What part of someone else makes you feel complete in a way you can't feel by yourself? I'm sure Robert (being the secure man that he is) wants his girl to have an opinion and to stand on her own name.

It's time to feel your inner strength and deal with what's next. Your strength lies in knowing that your bruised heart will heal.

You must set your mind to the fact that this is a short moment in your life. With time, prayer, and a gradual increase in self-esteem, things will shortly change for you. Decide that you will shift your attitude. You will entertain only positive thoughts toward yourself and everything else. When thoughts of your past relationship or your ex, or negative thoughts about you and your situation, arise, do not shun them. Instead, simply make a small effort to think of things that make you feel happy. If the thought of the car you purchased for your ex that put you in debt starts to stir up anger, that will only attract more thoughts to feed into your anger, and now you are angry for the next thirty minutes. Not only are you angry, but you are also tired and probably have had a full conversation in your mind about what you should have done or said and so forth. That is not the way to deal with such a sensitive topic. When a negative thought comes to mind, and you start to feel a painful emotion, simply switch to thinking about that scene in a movie that made you laugh, the next house you see yourself buying and how you want to decorate it, or the next trip you want to take. You might even go so far as to think about the next guy and the many things he will do to make you laugh. This is a simple way to switch your thoughts from negative to positive. In this way you train your thoughts to move forward, and you express to yourself how you no longer wish to live in that space of negativity. Where your mind settles, so does your heart, and if you truly want to change, you must start with your attitude.

Your attitude and feelings about others need to be reassessed. If you find yourself in a place of bitterness and resentment…let it go. Your hurt should not affect your relationship with the people around you. Those who truly love you do not want to see you snapping at others and being pissed off at the smallest things. You let bitterness go when you let God in. Take the time to surrender your feelings to him, and realize that though your feelings are valid, they should not serve as your prison sentence, since you are only hurting yourself and others.

No Man-Bashing

Being bitter and resentful can lead to cultivating a distaste for the opposite gender. Let me just say, gender hating is not attractive. You may be tempted to say the most inappropriate things about the male species and view them in a negative and undeserving light. This is called man-bashing. Refrain from doing this and taking part in conversations in which others are doing the same. The truth is, there are good guys and there are bad guys, just as there are good women and bad women. Man-bashing is not going to attract your future love. In fact, it will do the exact opposite and scare good ones away because of your ingrained attitudes about men. Not every man did to you what the last man did. Examine why you chose the men that you've dated. What is it about you that keeps attracting these types of men? What is it about them that intrigues you? Ask yourself if intrigue triumphs needs.

To put it simply, you do not attract what you want by stating what you dislike and dwelling on that. You welcome new change by talking about what you want and choosing to see the good in your situation. Maybe, if you are still struggling with your newfound singleness, you're asking, "What *is* good about my current situation?" It's all in your outlook. Now is the time to face your issues and learn from them. Now you can get yourself together. You are learning how to handle a loss at a different level, and you are finding your strength within it. Your outlook should be that next time you will get what you want and need. It's your chance to get better and not settle. Your outlook may also be a statement to yourself:

"I am out of that chapter of confusion and being given a fresh start" or "I can finally relax without unnecessary stress."

Setting Your Expectations

There should also be a change in your expectations. This means asking yourself what you expect for your future, your next relationship, and yourself. What do you feel is a must in your relationship? If you have taken one thing away from your last relationship, I'm sure it is your "do's and don'ts" and your "wills and won'ts." An example of some expectations could be: there must be trust, unconditional love, and the ability to open up and talk about everything in a judgment-free zone.

Trust could mean that you must be able to believe overall what your partner says to you. Unconditional love may mean that he values you, whether you are a CEO or an unemployed student. Being able to talk about anything in a judgment-free zone may mean that you can express yourself, from your fears to what excites you to your past mistakes, and still be deemed a woman of substance. This is what unconditional love looks like. These may not be your exact expectations, but you get the idea. These are realistic expectations, and though they may not make your future guy "the perfect guy," he will be the right guy for you in terms of what you want and need.

When setting expectations, you must allow room for them to be met in a way that's different from what you envisioned. There should be room for that slight margin of error, with the ability to work toward better. An example of this could be that you expect to always be respected in your relationship. Well, this is a very valid expectation, but what happens if your future partner makes a simple error that you consider offensive and disrespectful? Do you end it right there, or do you tell him that that particular action was disrespectful and that you will not tolerate it again, and then see where this leads?

Should You Have a List of Expectations?

If you're wondering if you should make a list of your expectations, the answer is no. You should not have a list of, say, fifty expectations you demand your future partner to live up to. You should have about three to five (or even less if you can) main ones that are crucial to you, and you should stick to them. Your expectations are personal. While they should not be superficial if you want a relationship of meaning, they are *your* expectations. You must also examine where you have gathered your expectations from and why. Many of our expectations come from our friends, family, society, and other external influences, but the truth is, you must be in sync with what resonates with you.

Your expectations should also be seeded in your development of self. What do you expect of yourself in terms of the direction you would like to move in, the actions you would like to take, and the feelings you would like to feel? Examples of expectations of yourself would be statements such as: "I expect to believe in my decisions and what I draw into my life" or "I expect to stick to what I know is right for my future, regardless of who or what enters my life and feels good right now."

Your ability to manage your expectations helps you step out of your comfort zone and experience change. With a different mind-set, your faith grows and the actions you take to elevate yourself increase as well.

Change Starts with Working on Yourself

Any change that happens starts within you. In fact, the only way you can see external changes is when you decide to make changes from within. You must want to do better and have better because you believe you are better than what you have accepted for yourself in the past. You have grown and can now accept that some changes need to be made. As fabulous as you are, you may have some characteristic that you can improve on. An example of this could be that you may not be as domestic as you would like to be. Maybe you want to learn to cook or make a habit of making your bed in the morning (even if you live alone).

In terms of character building, you may want to learn to embrace people and have more fun by hosting dinner parties and game nights. Or maybe you want to become more of an initiator and take a class, such as a dance class, that will help you be "that" person who takes charge. Improve in areas that would help you in your next relationship. Always remember that the most important traits to improve on are the ones that concern how you feel about yourself, your ability to care for others, and your skills — in that order. If your last partner complained about your lack of care, or your insecurities, or your ability to just say what you mean, then these are areas you should explore, without compromising the peacefulness of your spirit.

The only way your changes will really take root is if you continue to move forward until the actions become habits. In other words, the changes will only become normal to you through exposure and repetition, regardless of how you feel. At first you may find it easy to make the change, but after a few days or weeks your mind and body may reject the new thoughts and actions since they feel foreign. They will question why and try to fight off your new habits. And this is where it becomes tough. It's the same with going to the gym. You start off with good intentions, but eventually you give in to your mind telling you that this isn't you and that you should stay home and watch TV. You must have the willpower to overcome and keep going until both your mind and body accept your new actions and they become your new normal.

In the Act of Gratitude You Will Experience Change

Think of it this way. You are out of that relationship. Be grateful that you are out. Be grateful for what has been revealed to you. The pain you may be experiencing now is better than waking up every morning knowing your situation is not right but prolonging the inevitable. The pain of holding on is worse than the pain of letting go. As time goes by, you'll realize that there is a kind of joy in being set free from what you once thought was a slice of heaven (some days). This is the time to express your gratitude to God, your friends, and your family for supporting you through your tough times. While it is easy for you to feel angry and resentful, being grateful, with the focus on moving forward, will bring about a much easier transition to the next phase of your life. Through gratitude, you can usher in more positive feelings, turning even a bad relationship into a stepping stone to your path of freedom. This gives you the clarity and strength needed to get you through those not-so-easy days. By being grateful for people and things, you choose to see the positive in everything. This viewpoint will help you combat depression, feelings of isolation, and anger.

When you practice gratitude you almost immediately feel as if a weight has been lifted off your shoulders. You realize there is so much in your life to be thankful for. There is so much more out there in the world that you can and will love and that will love you right back. It's time to step up your gratitude game, especially when dealing with painful changes. Even in your darkest hour, there is always some light present. God never gives up on you or leaves you in your own mess. Whether you get out of the darkness kicking and screaming or praising and being grateful is a choice that only you can make. Love your way through every detail, and the healing process will soon be a piece of cake.

Elevating Your Beliefs

After any life-changing experience, old beliefs start to dissipate as a result of what you went through. This is the prime time to set a new direction for where you want to go spiritually, mentally, emotionally, and physically. If you're not big on using your imagination or entertaining the thought that anything is possible, then you might struggle a bit with these ideas. But limiting your thoughts and beliefs because of negative past experiences will keep you feeling the same feelings, doing the same things, and attracting the same people and situations into your life. You'll continually say, "I've been through this before." Why? Because you did not learn the lesson the first time. You did not make a conscious effort to believe in something new for yourself. Your old beliefs no longer serve. You may argue that what you believed before about yourself, your partner, or your relationship didn't play out so well, but I'm here to tell you that it did. After all, it was a new set of beliefs that made you leave (if you were the one to end the relationship).

What do you believe is to come forth for you? When it comes to your past, what belief did you hold on to that did not serve you? Who and what encouraged a belief that you no longer hold on to? Before you can take any action and make any commitment to yourself and others, you must be able to stand on a solid foundation of belief, one that cannot be budged, regardless of past circumstances.

While you might want to drop or readjust some beliefs, you must have a set that is truly nonnegotiable for you. You should not be able to easily abandon your beliefs just because things do not look good or something went wrong. Your beliefs need you to stand by them, regardless of what is going on. That is one way your beliefs show up and recognize you. Any type of change you are set on making in your life will always start with your beliefs and your commitment to them.

The Priority: Your Happiness

How important is happiness in your life? This may sound like a silly question, but the truth is, while you think you're chasing after happiness and freedom, you may have imprisoned yourself with ideas about the future instead of attending to yourself properly right now. Your happiness is a vital part of a healthy relationship with yourself and others. When you put yourself last and attend to someone else's happiness first, you are telling yourself that you are not worth it and that you don't deserve happiness. You are telling others you come second. The long-term effects can be devastating, since you may later latch on to the idea that your happiness is all that matters and then take it to the extreme by being overly selfish and unable to have healthy relationships with others.

When you decide to take care of yourself by feeding your mind, body, and spirit and by affording yourself the same level of respect you would give to your loved one, you'll find yourself doing less complaining, having more passion for life, and being less attached to what others do and what they say about you. You'll realize that although other people's words and actions can hurt you, at your core you are happy. It only gives way when you give it away. A lot of conflict with others happens when we are not happy with ourselves. You might be saying, "But making others happy makes me happy," and while that can be true, it is only a matter of time before your self-neglect takes its toll. There must be a balance to all that you do. The change that you seek moving forward rests in your ability to prioritize your own happiness.

Because happiness looks different to everyone, it's best to understand that what you accept as happiness for yourself should, on some level, be a sacred place for you. Whether you like to retreat by spending time meditating, reading, or painting your nails, you want to make sure that you attend to your happy place every single day. You get to your happy zone not only by practicing gratitude but by paying attention to your daily needs and attending to them. The priority you give your happiness has changed. It no longer depends on who has walked in and out of your life, nor should your happiness ever be on life support because of another person's beliefs about you. Taking care of yourself, inside and out, is now at the top of your to-do list.

EIGHT SIGNS THAT YOU ARE ON THE RIGHT PATH

9

You are on the road to recovery. It may not feel like it, but the truth is, you are doing much better than you were a year ago, a few months ago, even a few weeks ago. There will come a time when you won't even remember his name and will just shake your head at the foolishness you put up with. When you place yourself in positive environments and let go of the thoughts and feelings that no longer serve you, you will find that with time you will begin to feel better. You'll get back your happiness and start enjoying the simple things. The reality is that some days will be better than others. There will be days when you experience five different emotions, there will be days when you feel that you are completely over him, and there will be days when the breakup feels like it just happened. While you are healing, you can either leave it to time, or you can try to take charge of it.

When you decide to take charge, you'll learn that you cannot hide behind your emotions. You must face them. You'll face the fact that it is over and, regardless of what you do or don't do, it will *not* come back and be the relationship of your dreams. During the various stages of healing, you'll find the best avenue to let out your frustrations. You'll let them out more than once and probably say or write the same things over and over until you have desensitized yourself. You'll stop clinging to any hope for reconciliation and accept closure. Whether you received closure through conversation or just by accepting that the end of the relationship is closure enough, you will be in the right now and choose to surround yourself with people who motivate you to be the best version of yourself. Your recovery from a broken heart is a personal journey, and while you may believe that with each breakup it should get easier and easier, the truth is, it doesn't. Because every single breakup is different in terms of attachment and circumstances, there are also different levels of healing. When you have first healed spiritually and possess enough strength to function mentally, you will then be ready to heal physically. Let's take a look at these three levels of healing:

SPIRITUAL HEALING. Once you recognize that your source of happiness and life comes from the Most High, you will quickly learn that what feels like a loss is for your greater good and will be replaced with something better because of God's love for you. The connection you had with your ex is not greater than the love that God is inviting into your life now.

MENTAL HEALING. You'll realize that your thoughts have shifted off of what you thought you couldn't live without and onto what you now want for yourself. You'll recover from depression and any other forms of emotional trauma. You'll find the strength to make a new commitment to yourself not to settle for anything less than what you deserve.

PHYSICAL HEALING. Your physical symptoms, such as lack of energy, nausea, loss of appetite, and constipation, are all due to stress. These symptoms will subside with time as you improve spiritually and mentally. You may even come to the conclusion that you'll never put yourself in a position to experience this kind of stress again.

When you are dealing with a broken heart, the main goal is to deal with core issues, but the most immediate goal is to get over him and break the connection quickly. Here are eight signs that you are on the right path to getting over him:

SIGN 1: YOU NO LONGER CARE WHAT HE IS DOING. When mutual friends try to bring up your ex, you simply shrug off the conversation. You no longer check his social media accounts because you no longer care. If he shows up to your favorite Friday-night hangout spots, you are not bothered by it and go about having a good time as if he weren't there. Those late nights when you couldn't stop wondering if he was thinking about you or obsessing over who he was with are in the past. You have come to understand that it is no longer your concern, and you wish him the best.

SIGN 2: YOU HAVE THE OPPORTUNITY TO HURT HIM, BUT YOU CHOOSE NOT TO. Even the most poised and spiritually grounded woman can be pushed to do something she will regret later. Let's say, for example, that he entrusted you with some sensitive information. Instead of revealing it, you keep that information to yourself, even when you know you could hurt him with it. As you let time go by and your prayers are answered, your desire to seek revenge dissipates. You have excused his actions toward you, not for his sake but for yours.

SIGN 3: WHEN HE CALLS YOU, YOU DON'T RUSH TO ANSWER THE PHONE. In the past, every time the phone rang, you were hoping it was him. You would glance at your phone every few minutes, hoping for a text message, social-media update, or phone call, believing he'd just say something to make you feel better. He used to call you at least once a day, and you had to experience the withdrawal symptoms. Well, those days are over. Now when he wants to talk, you have little desire to hear what he has to say. You used to answer after the first ring, and now you miss calls because you're busy living. Returning his phone call is no longer a priority for you, since you've come to realize that he has nothing new to say and you don't care to waste your time.

SIGN 4: THE THOUGHT OF GETTING BACK TOGETHER NO LONGER APPEALS TO YOU. There was once a time when you believed the relationship could have been salvaged and that with just a few adjustments made by both parties, the issues could have been worked out. But that option wasn't available to you. He wanted to talk, but he didn't want to get back into a relationship that he felt needed some breathing room. It's a new day, and the topic of going back to what now seems like a toxic situation is no longer open for discussion. Now he wants to talk reconciliation, and just the thought of it makes your stomach turn. Now that you know what fresh air smells like, you are quite reluctant to go back to the staleness of your old relationship.

SIGN 5: YOU ARE NO LONGER INTO GAME PLAYING. At some point after the breakup, you may have done some things to try to get his attention or to expose the kind of guy he is. The possibility of his no longer having feelings for you just didn't make sense, so you played games to see how he would respond. Game playing is what a person does when she is hurt, wanting answers, and not able to move on, right? Well, no longer. Through time and acceptance, you no longer go out of your way to get his attention. You may have once been thinking and doing some crazy things that were not in your character, but not anymore. Now you take the high road.

SIGN 6: YOU CAN BLESS HIM AND MEAN IT. You were probably taking the high road when you chose not to respond to the outrageous accusations against you and the ridiculous temper tantrums, even when you were hurt by his actions. Yet even though you took the high road, it was still hard for you not to have any negative thoughts toward him and the situation. You prayed that the grudge you held would go away, and eventually it did. Now, when you pray for yourself, you also pray for his well-being. Those well wishes come from a sincere place, and there is no anger. He is no longer the enemy, and you are moving forward with a lighter heart.

SIGN 7: WHEN YOU HEAR HIS NAME, YOU DO NOT FEEL DISTRAUGHT. He had your heart, and it would jump every time he touched you, looked at you, or even said your name. At one point just hearing his name gave you butterflies. When the relationship came to an end, so did that feeling. Hearing his name after that horrible breakup no longer incited feelings of love but instead disappointment and depression. When you are moving forward in the right direction, you can hear his name and no longer be swayed. You can even say his name and be stress-free.

Sign 8: When you see him, he looks different. He may once have been your angel, but post-breakup you saw him as your enemy. But now after everything that has happened, he looks completely different to you. When you saw him in the past, you only saw hurt, anger, or from time to time that attractive man you once loved. Now all that's changed. Now you see a man whom you have forgiven and who is finding his way. What you thought was once an ugly and destructive soul, you now see simply as a soul, needing to love himself and recognize who he is as an individual.

This new you, this healed you, knows you will be more than okay. You now want the best for him as well as yourself. While from time to time you may think of the past, for the most part you are focused on yourself and on building your future. You are stronger, wiser, and better than ever. You have chosen you. Not only have you chosen yourself, but you have also chosen to accept whatever path your ex is on. You are moving forward.

 # 10 FINDING LOVE AGAIN

Y ou deserve a partner who respects you, cherishes you, honors you, preserves you, and prays for you. Now that you have made room for that, it's time to welcome love back into your life. You have a clean slate. Now that you are no longer tied to the pain, and loving yourself again feels oh so good, you are ready. You're ready for a divine companion. Now that you've healed, you realize that what you thought was a loss was actually a gain. It's time for you to expect better. Visualizing what you want and what love looks and feels like is a great way to get into the mind-set of attracting a new partner. It's time to start dating, and having fun again in the process.

While starting all over in the dating world once may have felt like a bore, now it should feel exciting, adventurous, and a bit liberating. Yes, you will have to slowly reveal who you are to others, and that can be scary when you feel vulnerable, but you also have the opportunity to meet new people, discover the world with new eyes, and do things you wouldn't have tried before, and you can filter out what works for you and what doesn't. Don't look at dating as a task. If you view it as a homework assignment or another chore you have been putting off, then you certainly are not in the right mind-set to date or to make the smartest decisions as you go. This is the time to just let go and renew your views on the process of gaining new friends and finding a partner. Yes, you'll probably encounter some who are nowhere near what's right for you. The process always involves this. When dating, the general rule is not to settle for the first guy you get to know. While you may not be a "dater" type of woman, it's best to date others before deciding to stick with the first guy you date. You want to make sure he's right for you rather than settling on him simply because you do not want to go on any more dates.

Again, this has everything to do with making the right decision, not just a decision that's convenient right now. If you are thinking long-term, then really give yourself the time to appreciate good company and be courted. Use the dating process as a way to work on your weaknesses with the opposite sex. If you have a hard time saying no, for example, then this is a great time to practice your ability to do just that, with no attachments. It is very important for you to remember that every moment of every date is short-lived until you decide to make more of it. You do not have to make any decisions that do not feel comfortable to you, and you are not under any obligation to compromise who you are and your happiness at any time.

The Open Heart

With an open mind comes an open heart. If you really believe that you are ready for love, then you must be willing to show that. That means the attitude, doubt, sarcasm, and any other negative attribute stemming from a failed relationship must no longer be present when you are making the effort to invite the love of new friends and of a new romantic interest into your life. Whatever you may have gone through in your past is not to be placed in someone else's hands. Your new beau should not have to pay the consequences for what someone else did to you or how that person made you feel. You are starting over. This is a renewal season for you, and you need an open heart and mind so that you can go through this process without feeling like it is a big drag. You have transformed and are in a special place of wanting and expecting better. Your new beliefs and mind-set have opened you up to exploring the world — which consists of more than seven billion people! You are ready to step out and enjoy life with new individuals.

When you are dating, give each individual a chance. Take the time to really listen to what he is saying, both verbally and nonverbally. An open heart means you carefully allow yourself to be vulnerable at the right times. You can comfortably tell someone what you want and what your long-term goals are, even if he does not match who you are. You can move on to the next person, knowing you are not attached. You do not make anyone your source of love, because you know God is your source; he loves you and you love yourself. An open heart also means you take risks and no longer hide behind your pain. It means trusting God to protect your heart while stepping out there and exploring what he has put in front of you. An open heart says that, despite the outcome, you know you are taken care of and that what you seek is every second coming closer. While you're dating, you have the opportunity to take the lessons you learned in past relationships and apply them. Opening your heart means allowing yourself to feel good again, to feel love again, and to accept what is, without forcing the process.

Where to Look for Love

When searching for love, don't go out trying to find it. Yes, I know this sounds ridiculous, but purposely trying to find love can cause frustration, since you are trying to control the process. *Stop looking*. What you truly want to attract is the love inside *you*. Stop searching for what's already there, and just have fun. Let your spirit guide you to a love that matches. I would love to tell you that you should go here, here, and here, and stay away from here, here, and that place too, but the truth is, love doesn't work like that. Attracting your next partner by controlling where you go will not work. If you have an instinct to go somewhere, then let God work, and go. This is a trusting process. You need to be open to possibilities when you are ready for them. While popular belief dictates that you should stay away from clubs if you're looking for a serious companion, the truth is, I would never tell you that. I'm telling you to have fun and let your love attract its match. Engage in activities that you enjoy, believing that you will attract someone who is into some of the same things that you are. If you're into foreign languages and take a foreign language class for fun or like to participate in international restaurant week, then this may be the place to attract like-minded people.

This isn't something forced or far-fetched. It's an extension of you. Look, if you are not a cook and believe standing by the produce section in a grocery store will get you an ideal guy, you just might be setting yourself up. If he thinks you can cook, and you truly can't or do not even like to, then you just put yourself in a sticky situation all because you wanted to control something that does not come naturally to you. Yes, you must put yourself out there, but not at the expense of who you are. You must remember that when you are looking for love, look directly at your source of love, which is God. When you can wake up every day smiling and feeling your relationship with God growing, your friendships blossoming, and your appreciation for your family deepening, you won't have to look hard for love. At the right time, love will find you, because you attracted it. If you want happiness in your life, make an effort to be happy every day, and you can expect it to come at any moment without your even thinking about it. You've heard over and over again that faith without works is dead; put in the work by showing up to places, and be open to it. Think about what you are inviting to come to you.

Expect the Unexpected

You may find your companion in the most unexpected way. There is no blueprint for finding the right one. You may not be open to online dating, but don't rule it out. Also, you may never have dreamed that your future companion turns out to be one of your closest friends, a neighbor, or someone you've helped. It can happen. Dating is exactly how Forrest Gump described the box of chocolates: *You never know what you're going to get.* Expecting the unexpected simply means not to pre-decide what your mate needs to look or act like. It means not expecting him to be anything he is not so that he fits what you want. If you see who he is, and you don't like it, you are not bound to him. Open yourself up to different types of people. If you kept to the same type of guys for the past ten years, it may be time to reevaluate why you are not open to "that type" and how "your type" may just not be for you. Don't let your interest in one type of man keep you from meeting the one who is truly meant to connect and grow with you. If it hasn't worked out the past few times that you tried your type, why would you give it another chance? Why not open yourself up to someone who can help you explore untapped parts of yourself?

The truth about the unexpected is that it can lead to exactly what you expect in a relationship. He may not look or act like what you're used to, but he can love you in the way you want and need to be loved. Unconditional love does not bind itself to conditions of the human mind.

Finding Love within Your Circle

Right now you may be in a good place, or getting to that good place. Your relationship with your family is the best it can be. You have the right friends, and you are truly at peace with where things are going in your life. As I said above, there is no blueprint for finding love. You should always remain open to wherever love comes from (granted that it was delivered by God). It is never a good idea to limit the ways you expect God to deliver your love to you. Let God make it fitting for your purpose.

One of the many ways you can meet your "next" is through family. Your family knows you best. Your family members may be the perfect individuals to introduce you to who they think is right for you, based on who they know you to be. This can actually be a relief to you if you have an eclectic group of siblings, cousins, and elders. If he already knows your family and enjoys their company, then it just makes it easier for you. Your family is just one avenue that love can take to enter your life.

Another avenue could be through your friends and social events. Your friends may be an amazing source. Don't be so quick to tell them no when they offer to hook you up with a "potential." Of course, if you truly feel like nothing good can come from dating your friend's friend or coworker, then of course do not proceed. But remember, your job is to be open to the ways that love can come to you. This is a life of taking chances, not living in confinement. You have the opportunity to explore your world and all that it comprises. If you believe your friend knows you well enough to pick a good match for you, why close yourself to this opportunity? Even if you are an introvert, this is all part of the process. If you choose to keep your process private, then you limit your options. If you are really open to the many paths that love can travel on its way to you, remember that you have some avenues right within your reach.

One advantage of meeting your potential partner through friends is that you can do so at a social event, which takes the pressure off. Use activities not only to meet whomever your friends choose to introduce to you but also other suitors as well. Remember, you can meet anyone anywhere: networking events, concerts, holiday parties, and so on. Know that you might meet your next partner anywhere. What is required of you is to just show up, love yourself, and make the most of any situation you find yourself in. Walk into a room feeling loved and taken care of, and you will make better decisions for yourself.

It Happens on Its Own Divine Timing

You may kiss a lot of frogs before you find your prince, but that doesn't mean that those frogs can't turn out to be amazing friends. Even in the process of dating, or maybe especially in this process, you cannot force divine timing. Based on how you meet or the things you say to each other, you will know that some people are just meant to help steer you toward the right path, make your journey to the right person feel incredible, or help you find a person who will teach you unforgettable lessons. When you choose to let go of all control, you will enjoy the benefits of divine timing. There is no feeling greater than allowing God's time and all those unplanned things to happen to you. You'll witness what you've prayed for played out in a more special way than you ever could have orchestrated on your own. It is through your belief in divine timing that you turn your expectations to reality. Recognize that all the frogs you may kiss can lead you to an experience customized by the Most High that you will never forget. During the dating process, it may seem as if your match is not out there or that he just doesn't exist. You may find yourself not connecting with anyone and wondering when and where it will finally happen. You can only discover the answer to this in your expectation that what you want and need is in you, surrounds you, and is coming closer to you. To think anything less simply sets you back in receiving what you ask for.

The sooner you open yourself to dating and learning about people with no judgment, the sooner you will begin the process of finding love and of inviting divine timing to take its course. You can never rush a process, nor should you want to, since you want to get the full benefits of what you learn along the way. As you actively seek to attract a new love interest, you will come to understand that whoever and whatever appeared to you in the process was there to help you grow, to show you another part of yourself, and to prepare you for your "next." Divine timing doesn't require anything from you but to show up for the things and people that you want. Anything contrived by you or anyone else may have a tougher time working out, if it is not founded in God.

You cannot force something or someone to be or do what they are not meant to be or do. You may have experienced something like this in your past relationship if you were asked to do things that were not you. But as you begin to date, there is no need to feel less than or not good enough for another person, since you are molded by God's hands for the divine man to come into your life at the divine time.

Entertaining Potential Suitors

You will encounter potential suitors who will wine and dine you, and you'll have to choose one to spend more time with and eventually call your own. Your potential guy could come from anywhere, and if you are actively opening your life and environment to welcoming your new guy, then you will make the necessary adjustments. You might start taking different routes to work, going places where you'll meet new people, trying different foods, exploring different neighborhoods, and simply allowing your instinct to guide you when you get the urge to do something different. When sorting out your suitors, you may look for qualities such as respect, attentiveness, honesty, and loyalty. What's important in turning a potential suitor into the one you call yours is having similar core values and life goals. When you are able to openly speak about what you want with a future partner, and your partner expresses the same things, then you can move forward, establishing a relationship confidently.

What They See in You

For each date you go on in which you are talking, laughing, and enjoying each other's company, you may wonder what your date looks for and sees in you. Sure, you are an amazing, confident, got-her-stuff-together woman, but what does he see in you when you are together? Although the answer to this question depends in large part on the individual, I will generalize by saying that whatever motivates you to look for a partner will be visible to others. For example, if you want a man with money, most men will be able to tell if you are after their wallet. If you are baby ready, most men will also sense that about you. Whatever it is you are desperately wanting, he will most likely be able to intuitively see it, and he will either gravitate toward it or back down from it. If you project love and a spirit of peace, then your potential will want to make dating you a priority, if he favors this in his life as well. If you love to talk about yourself or your ex, your potential could think you are in need of attention and not yet over your past hurt.

You have reached a point where you have decided to get back on track. Your focus is having a growing relationship with God, with yourself, and with those around you. When you are truly growing in these areas, your potential suitors will only be able to see light, joy, and confidence, and even a potential home with you. Those you date may be able to see any flaws you try to hide and may love them better than you do, because they know they're what makes you you. Some suitors will be able to step up in places where you are weak and protect you. Depending on where you are in your relationship with God and yourself, your perspective on life and insights about particular people and situations will amaze those you are dating. When your potential sees you happy, he will want to continue making you happy and to keep that smile on your face.

In a world where we are all wanting a place to escape to and just be ourselves, your companion wants a place to call home. If you both decide to be in a relationship with each other, then there is no need to question whether he finds you special. When there are clear signs that your potential is making room in his life for you to feel welcomed and continue to shine, you can most certainly believe that he sees you as a special woman in his life. If there are discussions of honesty, vulnerability, trust, and consideration, and acts that demonstrate these things, then there is no need to doubt what you prayed for in your life. He sees you as you are. You may doubt this because of your treatment in past relationships, but the truth is, he sees what he can be with you. Remember that whatever you are feeling is what is being projected. If you are feeling unworthy and meek, then anyone you date will be able to see that and will have to decide if those are qualities he really wants in a potential partner.

Why Do Some People Attract a Partner Faster Than Others?

You may be wondering why some individuals are able to recover after a breakup and attract their next romantic interest faster than others. It just seems to come so effortlessly to them. In fact, you may have been that person who gets into one relationship after the next, easily segueing between them. Well, there is a difference between being able to pick up and move into your next relationship, only to repeat the same patterns, and dating men who are worthy of your love. Your faith kept your vision clear, and even when you couldn't see the evidence, you knew it was there. Attracting fast really is relative. What may seem like fast to you may not be fast to someone else. You do not really know how long this person has been practicing positive thoughts and making room for what she truly wants. She could easily tell you she didn't do anything (and she probably is not conscious of what she's doing, outside of prayer), but the truth is that it's not about what she's doing; it's about what she's not doing. For example, one of the biggest factors in attracting a partner is having no resistance to what is coming. What this means is that they don't entertain any doubts, what-ifs, or negative thoughts about what might be brought to them. If you keep questioning the delivery of your "next," then you are sending mixed signals about what you want and who you trust. You are displaying to yourself and to God your disappointment in your lack of control; you're introducing your fears into the situation. Those who are able to attract faster have relinquished all control and are able to trust that it is all in the right hands. These individuals believe in not forcing things to happen. They are able to understand that in the right time and under the right circumstances things will play out for the good.

When you can stand confidently in who you are, you no longer waste your time forcing situations or conversations that cannot happen naturally. Those who attract faster are not busy looking for the same type of guy but rather are open to the *right* type of guy. These same individuals who attract faster are the ones who are expecting but not looking. As I've stated, expectation is knowing that what is yours is already here and belongs to you. When you know this, there is no need to act as if it is missing and you cannot find it. It is already here, and in due time, you will be able to love it. Those individuals who attract love quickly know that what they have asked for in prayer and have thanked God for has already presented itself and is making its way into their world. They have created a mind-set of expecting (not forcing) and simply believing. They are also ready to receive what they asked for, and so they bring in what they call for more naturally. You can practice this mind-set as well, and you will see how quickly new love comes to you.

11 HOW TO WELCOME LOVE

Putting yourself out there in the hopes of finding your love companion, after all you've been through, may sound crazy, but it's not impossible. In fact, it's quite possible, depending on where you are in your healing process, and on your faith, beliefs, and attitude. The process of bringing love into your life requires you to transform your thoughts about deadlines into the belief that love has walked into your life. I've spoken about God's divine timing, and you must understand that you do not and cannot micromanage God in the hows and whens of your wants and needs being fulfilled. This process requires you to fully trust that it works. If you are an introverted person, this is going to require you to step out of your comfort zone and take a bit more of a hands-on approach. Start partaking in activities that are outside your residence and place of employment. Don't spend every day that you are out looking for love, but instead allow yourself to *feel* the love you want. Loving yourself is the golden ticket to attracting a loving partner into your life. The process of bringing in your love allows no room for doubt or desperation. If either of these feelings is present in your actions and speech, then you may be impeding your efforts to attract love. There are three love actions you should engage in every single day, in a joyous and peaceful state of expecting:

1. Create the vision.
2. Invite the man you envision into your heart.
3. Tell God thank you, and rejoice in receiving.

The vision of what love looks and feels like to you must be in your mind every day. It's very simple. Play with thoughts about what you would do as a couple, about how he would show you love every day, and vice versa. Imagine how he makes you smile, what he says to you, how the two of you meet — without holding on to the expectation that it has to happen that way but knowing it will happen in *some* way. You want to be just like a kid who still believes in things like the tooth fairy as you go about your day in expectation. When you have fun with this, it shows on the outside and should distract you from any doubts you may have. Believe that you can have it, and it is yours. After all, it is your vision. Your vision should make you smile, laugh, feel good, and generate more good thoughts. Do not compare your past with your vision, but simply let your vision be what you believe it can be in your life. You can guide your vision any way you would like, just as long as you realize that what you see for yourself is what you'll bring into your life. If you don't like what you see, quickly change it, because once you see him, you must invite him into your space.

This is the "act as if" part. How much of an active role does your new partner play in your life, and you in his? For example, if you believe that every day after work he stops by your place, then act as if he is doing that now. Go ahead and cook for two, put on the music you believe he would like or a channel you believe your new guy would be into. Instead of doing for one, do for two. Speak as if he is already there with you now. Make him a part of your life, and invite him into your space, because you are expecting him. As you see him in your vision, act as if he is already there, thanking God for him every day. And I mean *every day throughout the day*. Remember, this is the person you want, and you have him now, so tell God thank you. Thank him in advance for what you asked for. Thank him for everything your new guy does and says. Thank God for your man showing up at the right time. Thank God for a healthy relationship. Be grateful for the place you are in now. The present moment must feel good to you. It must be amazing for you. For while you want what you are asking for, you must also be able to appreciate where you are now. Be grateful that you know what you know and can move forward. Feel happy and full of excited anticipation. You do not need to curse what you went through or the fact that you're not where you want to be, since that will not bring in what you want. Since you are in a place of feeling good and alive, you are dwelling where God is. He is a feel-good God! God is love, and in knowing this, you can rejoice in your receiving. Your expectation is the spiritual alarm that says you know without a doubt that you are receiving what you asked for. Regardless of what it looks like, what happens, or what is being said, nothing can cloud your vision or shift your expectation. Take the time to rejoice each day in your receiving.

Prepare. Expect. Commit.

As I've stated many times now, love comes to you when it comes *from* you. What this means is that you must give whatever you are wanting. You must get rid of the selfish mind-set that this is only about receiving love. If you are one who does tit for tat, or keeps tabs on what someone does in comparison to what you do, then this isn't going to work for you. Being needy is not a way to attract a healthy, loving relationship into your life. That leans more in the direction of looking for someone to be dependent on rather than building a relationship with someone because of who he is. To attract your lover, you must demonstrate to those around you that you are a willing giver and not just a taker. A potential lover will feel like you have a lot to provide to others. Being a giver is also a sign of blessing and abundance. No matter what you do and how much you give, you will always be blessed. You will always attract in your life, and no one can take that away from you. Now, who wouldn't want to be around someone like that?

Givers who focus on providing love in a healthy, natural way do not have to worry about getting for themselves. The more you give of yourself, the more you get. Remember that most people want to give love and have their love reciprocated. You want to love someone who makes you feel lovable, and vice versa. When you are in the process of attracting love, be the one who gives attention, respect, compliments, and assistance. Each day find a way to stretch yourself and give. Do not just give from the comfort of your own home. Get out and give of yourself to people you may not know. Give your time, lend an ear, offer a skill, or just show appreciation. Explore your city, go for a walk, visit a zoo, or just take a moment to revel in nature, and imbue each day with the love God gives to you. When you make the conscious decision to give and make it a daily habit, not only will you attract the love of another who gives to you as well, but you'll grow to love yourself even more. Be willing to give in ways that you have been holding yourself back from. Your restrictions on giving have possibly placed restrictions on receiving.

Becoming Attractive

Don't fool yourself into thinking that looks don't matter. Do personality and personal attributes matter? Yes. Can any one of these survive on their own? No. That's my answer to you, and I'm sticking to it. When you initially meet someone, you do not have the luxury of learning all about their personal attributes if they do not get past the initial attractiveness phase for you. You can deny it all you want, but take the time to think about it…this rule applies to everything. Even when you go shopping at the grocery store, before you put that apple in your cart, you examine it. You don't know how it tastes, but you judge it by how it looks. We see a man before we get to know who he is. So yes, looks will always matter. Let's say you got the looks department down. You're an attractive woman physically, and you have made the effort to take care of yourself. So what's going on inside? What is it that men want to see that radiates from you? Well, a few things that would help you attract love would be to exhibit enthusiasm, be carefree and intelligent, and exude femininity and attentiveness. During this process of expecting love, be the woman who inspires those around you with your enthusiasm for life, your carefree nature, and the appreciation you have for the smallest gestures.

Many men will find you attractive when you are comfortable in your own femininity and you are attentive to your surroundings. For example, when you are out on a lunch date, put down your phone, and be confident in the opinions you express. Being able to communicate your thoughts, whether or not you agree with him, is another attractive trait. A woman who has good manners, says thank you, tones down the cursing, and consistently has a positive attitude is also deemed attractive.

Becoming attractive is not only about the things you do; it is also about who you are. If your goal is to attract something different from what you're used to, then you'll want to do things differently. You'll want to focus on what you want and bring yourself to feel and be on the level of your desires. If your desired "next" is an optimistic man who is a leader in business and among his friends, and you are a bit of a pessimist, then it's time to get on the same level. That means understanding how an optimistic person feels and how a leader functions, and incorporating those qualities if this person is truly what you want to attract. You tend to gravitate to those who understand what you are saying and what you have gone through. Likewise, if you want love to gravitate toward you, then you must bring yourself to the level of what you want; that is, you must reflect what love means to you in your actions and words.

A Confident Woman

"I used to walk into a room and wonder if people would like me. Now I walk into a room and wonder if I will like them."

As you plan to spend your time feeling loved, expect to receive with confidence. What this means is not only to fully trust in God to give you what you asked for but to feel assured that whatever you believe about yourself will be reflected in your life. The guy you attract will be attracted to the love you have for yourself and for the people and things you value. When you are firm in your beliefs and display a passion for your career, your loved ones, and the causes you hold dear, then the right guy will respect this and want to learn more. Your confidence will grow when you accept who you are and who you are becoming. When you have accepted your flaws, your weaknesses, and your strengths as part of your unique story and have decided that you are your own best friend, your confidence will know no bounds. When you are happy in your own skin, when you no longer need anyone's approval of the things you say and do or of how you look, you will attract the perfect love into your life.

A confident woman knows she is blessed and is a blessing.

She makes eye contact, walks straight and with a purpose, speaks up and doesn't hesitate with her decisions, and can take compliments without rejecting them. As a confident woman, you should take pride in yourself and how you look. When a negative thought enters your head about you or anyone else, you quickly decline entertaining it. You know how to highlight your positive traits and can discuss your likes, loves, and passions without dominating the conversation. A confident woman is able to do all these things without making another person feel inferior, showing off, overselling, or name dropping. When you operate out of confidence, you do not negotiate your boundaries. You are a reflection of love and the foundation of self-respect. Throughout the day, your attitude and demeanor summon what you are reflecting within yourself. You can see, by who and what comes into your life, how you feel within yourself. When you can confidently expect someone great to walk into your environment, then you move about your day with joy and at peace, able to enjoy whatever space you're in. You are able to sift through what you want and don't want. Your confidence has brought you out of desperation and into expectation.

Loving Like God Loves

"Loved them to the last and to the highest degree."

— JOHN 13:1 (AMPC)

There are many different levels of loving and being loved. As human beings, we all want the same thing, and that is to be loved at the highest level. We want it so much that we'll do almost anything to get it, whether that means altering our appearance, doing things that are not within our character, or sacrificing what we once deemed sacred to us. Throughout this book, I have talked about self-love and the love of God. When you are able to understand that the unconditional love God has for you is more than enough and that self-acceptance attracts even more for you to love about yourself, you can then bring forth a love from others that strengthens you. But the time you spend getting your "next" to come into your world requires you to love like no other. This means to display from the inside out an uncanny love toward others that you may not ever have thought was within you. But just as God lives within you, so does this love. There are times when our love has its limits. It becomes very conditional. You may need someone to do or say something before you are willing to do something yourself from a loving place. This is a self-serving type of love. It falls more along the lines of "If it doesn't serve you, then you can't serve it" or "What's in it for me?" Jesus taught his unconditional love in many ways that did not directly benefit him. He was a king who washed others' feet. I could go on, but you can get an idea of his love through what he has done in your life and how he has spared you. You're probably wondering what this has to do with your process of welcoming love into your life. Well, everything. When you operate from the highest level of love, you project into the world that no matter what happens to you, you will believe in the best for yourself and others. You choose to forgive easily and to no longer live outside of love. You are able to call forth your desires because love presides over them. When you love as God loves, you are living in his peace and are not distracted by anything or anyone who wants you to live any other way. When you love as God loves, your "next" will feel safe and witness the power of God and the peace in you. He will want to be in your presence because he will experience love and happiness and will reflect that back to you. This love, God's love, cures dysfunctional, unhealthy relationships. When you decide to start bringing in the love you desire, put your mind, spirit, and body in a place to serve and love unconditionally. If this is unnatural for you, then you need to do it every day of your life until it becomes a part of you. You are not to watch and compare what others are doing for you. Love makes amends, and if that is what it takes for you to move forward, then that is the action to take. There are no other acceptable actions. Love does not take a backseat to pride and ego. It is the living heart of the spirit.

NINE SIGNS YOU'VE
GOT A GOOD ONE

Moving forward never felt so good. Maybe a year ago you never could have imagined yourself being in this position, and I hope this book has helped you to heal and to turn your self-love toward welcoming true love into your life. The exciting time is here! It's exciting because you realize you have the power to make the right choices. It feels good to no longer feel hurt or be tempted to numb yourself to the pain. Let's face it, this is a happier you. You've not only accepted that your past relationship is over and may have been un-healthy for you, but you also understand that it had to happen so that you could get to this place of becoming stronger and open to what God has in store for you. All the sifting and sorting you've done between what you want and don't want makes your experience with others a bit more of an adventure for you.

Now you're dating again. Someone has been doing his best to get your attention, and you are enjoying it. You like how you feel and what you see, but you want to make sure you have a good one on your hands. I mean, we all know that we put our best foot forward when we are "applying" for a position at a company, and this scenario is no different. There is a gentleman who wants that position in your life, and you are currently interviewing. So after a few coffee shop meet-ups, dinner dates, and hour-long phone conversations, you really want to believe that this is a good match for you. While time, consistency, and effort will determine that, there are nine signs to look for that indicate you've got a good one on your hands.

HE WANTS TO SOLVE YOUR PROBLEMS. He doesn't want to see you hurting in any way, nor does he want you to be dissatisfied, so he takes on the role of being your problem solver. Now, this isn't a man who wants to control your life or dominate every aspect of it and your reactions to it. He is a man who wants you to live at ease. One of his goals is to make you happy, and he believes he can make your life easier by simply coming up with solutions. While you may want someone who will simply listen to you when you are upset, your love interest believes that if he listens deeply to you and then comes up with a solution, everything will be better, just like that. He wants to be your superhero. This is one of his ways of showing you that he cares.

HE CONSULTS WITH YOU. Before making any decisions, he consults with you. He wants to keep you in the loop with what is happening in his life. Whether he is offered a new job promotion, wondering if he should get the black or blue BMW, or trying to figure out what to do for his mother's birthday, he wants you to be a part of his life and to stay informed. He believes you make great decisions and wants you to be happy with the choices he makes.

HE TAKES AN INTEREST IN YOUR INTERESTS. Instead of shying away from the unknown, he is more than happy to learn about you, and he does that by taking an interest in your interests. He is curious to know what your passions are and why you are drawn to them. He wants to be exposed to your world. He remains curious about the causes, events, and hobbies that light you up and command your attention. Just as he wants you in his world, he also wants to be invited into yours.

HE MAKES PLANS. He does not have a problem being the initiator. He is actually one of those guys who takes the time to plan a romantic evening, suggest an activity, and put his ideas into action. He respectfully asks if you are available and makes plans to impress you. It may or may not be perfect, but it's the thought that counts. He doesn't just assume you are just a "Netflix and chill" kind of woman (nothing wrong with that from time to time); he makes the effort to spend time with you and show you other aspects of himself.

HE IS TRANSPARENT. You do not have to figure out what he's up to or who he's hanging out with, and you don't have to get confused about his stories, because he is transparent. He is very clear about what he is doing and his intentions. With him, there are no hidden messages or reasons for confusion, since he has nothing to hide from you. His transparency brings you security and enables you to believe in the relationship.

HIS FAMILY AND FRIENDS KNOW YOU. You are not being kept a secret. He has gladly introduced you to his family and friends as "his girl." You are not just another girl that his family and friends get to know, but you are "that girl" whom everyone hears about. He wants everyone important in his life to know who he is spending his time with and that you are important to him. When it comes to big family events and holidays, he wants you there. He's not afraid to flaunt you, because he is proud to be with you.

HE INCLUDES YOU IN HIS INTERESTS. He loves going to the opera, and he wants you there. He's part of the city basketball team, and he wants you to come to his games. He makes it a point to attend job-related networking events and wants you to be a part of them. From hiking, working out, and traveling to fixing up cars, he wants you by his side. He believes you bring him just as much joy (if not more) as spending time doing the things he loves. By choosing to introduce you to his world, he is showing you that he wants you to be a part of it.

HE LISTENS TO YOU AND RESPECTS YOUR OPINION. Your thoughts and opinions are important to him. When you speak, he is actively listening. He loves to ask you about your views on particular topics and is curious about how you think. He pays attention to your likes and dislikes and wants you to know he is taking your thoughts seriously. Because of his trust in you, he readily accepts your requests, within the parameters of your relationship, because he knows you only want to elevate your partnership with him.

HIS LIFE WITH YOU IS A FACTOR IN HIS DECISIONS. Sometimes amazing opportunities come up and quick decisions need to be made. It may be that there is a better job opportunity in another state or that he now has the chance to move into a bigger place that would cost more money. Maybe he wants to extend his education at a prestigious school that would give him the opportunity to advance his skills and open his own business. Regardless of what comes up, he factors in his relationship with you in making the best decision for himself. It's no longer just about him; it's about having you with him and you being proud of him. He is careful not to jeopardize his life with you, while still taking advantage of good opportunities. If you keep these signs in mind when you start dating again, you will greatly increase your chances of making a good match. I wish you luck!

Now that you have reached the end of the book, you are ready to set out with a heart full of hope. You understand your value and you no longer dwell on what didn't work out but trust in God's plan for you, no matter what has transpired. You are not forgotten or being punished. Rather, you are loved, valued, and being molded, despite how the process of healing from a breakup and rediscovering yourself feels. Whether you have to go through this process two or three more times or never again, you are now equipped with the tools to get through tough situations and eventually reach your bliss. I wrote this book because past experiences have taught me that you are not meant to be brought down and kept there. It is time to embrace the truth that things do not happen to you, but for you. You can get everything you want and need from love.

ABOUT THE AUTHOR

Tatiana Jerome turned her personal experience into not just a thriving online presence but also a self-published book and a career counseling women and speaking at a variety of organizations. She lives in Florida.

www.tatianajerome.com

Facebook: www.facebook.com/iamtatianajerome

Twitter: @tatianajerome

Instagram: tatiana.jerome